HOSPITIOUS ADOPTION

JAMES L. GRITTER

Foreword by Randolph Severson

Arlington, VA

CWLA Press is an imprint of CWLA. CWLA is the nation's oldest and largest membership-based child welfare organization. We are committed to engaging people everywhere in promoting the well-being of children, youth, and their families, and protecting every child from harm. All proceeds from the sale of this book support CWLA's programs in behalf of children and families.

CWLA HEADQUARTERS
2345 Crystal Drive, Suite 250
Arlington, Virginia 22202-4815
www.cwla.org

CURRENT PRINTING (last digit)
10 9 8 7 6 5 4 3 2 1

Cover and text design by Tim Murren
Edited by Meghan Williams

Printed in the United States of America

ISBN: 978-1-58760-123-1

Library of Congress Cataloging-in-Publication Data

Gritter, James L., 1950-
  Hospitious adoption / James L. Gritter ; foreword by Randolph Severson.
    p. cm.
  Includes bibliographical references.
  ISBN 978-1-58760-123-1 (pbk. : alk. paper)
  1. Open adoption. 2. Adoptive parents. 3. Birthparents. 4. Adoption. I. Title.

HV875.G753 2009
362.734--dc22

2009000794

This book is dedicated to Dick Beachnau, a man of boundless grace and hospitality. An administrator who had the goodwill, respect, and courage to notice, listen to, and make room for idealistic young social workers, he created a culture in which amazing things could happen.

TABLE OF CONTENTS

FOREWORD

It is hard to write a foreword to a book whose candor and clarities are so revealing of a private resolve, of what has been generally intended and practiced but never truly identified, much less so artfully anatomized, so usefully and comprehensively described. One must feel a bit exposed, a trifle envious, but entirely grateful. These feelings, I suspect, I'll share with many readers of *Hospitious Adoption*.

The hardship is worth enduring because adoption is such important work. Adoption touches millions of people, literally, but *touches* is hardly the word; adoption, its aches and its intimacies, grabs, grips, crushes sometimes, and always shakes those who find themselves involved in it as triad member or professional, to the farthest reaches of their foundations. It's volcanic in intensity, seismic in effect. The sad fact, however, is that some people don't know it, or more truly said, deny it, and as a result—whether as birthparent, cowering in shame and secrecy; or adoptive parent, hoping that love is enough and will heal all wounds; or as adopted people, trying to persuade someone, not least of all themselves that "my adoptive parents are my only real parents"; or as professionals maintaining their objectivity—live quiet lives of alias identities.

It has been said that God created the world because he loved a good story. He must love adoption, because adoption makes a whale of a good story. Adoption throws into sharp relief so many of our ultimate concerns and worst failings as human beings—abandonment, suffering, loss, separation, the soul and body split, sex, illegitimacy, orphanhood, power, society, imagination, men and women, mystery, soul searching, reunion—so that they can be known not in the abstract, but with a human face and story.

Adoption is an important work and this book goes to the heart of adoption, where the author maintains hospitality resides. Hospitality may be at the heart of humanity too, the defining feature of what makes us human, just lower than the angels as the Bible says. Humanity not so much as worker or wise, but hospitable man, the animal able to lift himself above the other animals by the virtue of showing hospitality to the stranger, even the enemy. Even amidst the worst kinds of conflicts, the most vicious of divisions, human beings seem astonishingly capable of suspending for a moment their grievances and feuds, even their age-old hates, of stepping beyond their normal roles and into a larger self through acts, small and great, of hospitality. I think of a scene from Faulkner's *Flags in the Dust*, when Bayard—the Southern archetype of the lost generation, home from World War I; decadent, cursed by survivor's guilt, hurtling and sinking into headlong self-destruction and unreachable despair, incomprehensible to his aging aristocratic Sartoris family—flees through the woods, running away from something, frankly, when on Christmas Day he enters into the home of a black family preparing to sit down for their Christmas dinner. From the outside, to the person of Bayard's race and rank, the home would normally be almost invisible, a shack in the woods; but once he is graciously invited to cross its threshold, it is a home where Christ's birth is being celebrated with all due honor in a dinner that represents the best the house can offer. As Bayard begins to eat, he realizes that the mother and father are waiting for him to eat first, but he overrides their objections so that they all sit down, the mother and father and children, to dine together. They break bread together in a fleeting act of human communion that defies stored-up evils and leaves only Jim Crow standing at the door.

The conflicts and divides of adoption, the clashing needs and competing urgencies, are sometimes as wide and apparently impossible to bridge as those that divide the races. But as this book shows, hospitality can close the gap, can make that bridge, and further it shows us practically, concretely, and specifically how to do it. This is one adoption book that does not pretend that adoption isn't controlled by administrators and board members and others even more removed from actual casework who legitimately worry about economy, efficiency, productivity, and the bottom line. There is advice aplenty here too for such usually invisible folks.

The author's special focus is open adoption. *Open adoption* is not a term I'm particularly fond of. I'd rather just speak of adoption. Far from being an innovation of any kind, open adoption is simply a return to timeless and traditional forms of child-raising, a harkening back to the idea that—despite the assertions of both former Senators Hillary Clinton and Rick Santorum—it is neither a village nor a family that it takes to raise a child, but a village of families, and families come in every size, shape, and color of love. Perhaps the phrase *closed adoption* will eventually simply drop out of the language, not only the practice but the term itself falling into desuetude, along with other nightmares inflicted upon us by the social engineers of the 20th century who believed—sometimes blamelessly but more often for unconscionable but never-admitted reasons, having to do with increase of power—that human nature was a blank slate upon which they could inscribe their vision of what humanity was and could be. The idea of hospitality takes us back to human nature, to what it really is (which is sometimes execrable), but what it can also sometimes be. The key is to accept people for who they are, with tolerance and compassion, but not without an unflinching honesty about where we, and they, fall short, while inspiring them through word and deed. The word is hospitality and the deed is to host, with all the religious depth that this phrase evokes.

This is a gracious book written by a gracious man, who himself embodies the old verity he writes about hospitality. For over two decades he and his friends have hosted a conference in Traverse City in springtime, on the shores of Lake Michigan, when the cherry blossoms start to bloom. As this book goes to the heart of adoption, so that conference has gone to the heart of what a professional conference is meant to be. The Traverse City Conference on Open Adoption has been less of a conference and more of a retreat, in an almost radiantly spiritual sense, to which the whole of the open adoption community has made a biannual pilgrimage to partake of James Gritter's hospitality. What Jim's (if I may presume upon the courtly familiarity in which, in exhibiting, he inevitably invites) hospitality has always most inspired are spirited conversations, movable feasts of words, 'big ideas' put forth in the charm of friendly and welcoming cadences. This book has the rhythm and scope of one of those conversations: Jim, miles ahead of the rest of us, comes up with one of those big ideas, and casually offers it, as would a host. As the rest of us chime in, we realize gradually that he's been puzzling and pondering on this subject for years, maybe decades; read reams of materials in addition to every book on the subject; tested every notion and refined it more thoroughly through his communions with clients; and has come to something quite amazing, yet he continues to be willing—eager, even—to be instructed, to be 'guest,' to be enriched by other views and experiences. Reading Jim's words instead of hearing them has given us a chance to slow the pace, to extend the time and linger, to really take it all in, and experience the breadth, depth, and beauty of Jim's genius as he undertakes an extraordinary adventure about what is perhaps the most important idea in adoption work: hospitality.

Accept his most hospitable invitation to read this book. I have. I have already returned to its pages more than once and plan to go back again as I went back repeatedly to Traverse City, to return each time renewed, more hospitable to the soul of the work we do, to the heart and soul of adoption.

Randolph Severson PhD

INTRODUCTION

It's possible that Father Tom Brosnan is off his rocker. Mind you, I'm not doubting his brilliance, erudition, eloquence, or sense of humor—anybody who knows him is aware of all that—but I have reason to believe that this priest, who coincidentally is adopted, is also a bit daft. My suspicion stems from a comment he made a few years back while celebrating an ecumenical religious service at an adoption conference in Colorado. He was encouraging those who had gathered to be good to each other when he remarked, "Maybe we can be like Jim Gritter, who has been a good Samaritan to adoptees and birthparents through the years."

It is the nicest thing anyone has ever said about me. I mean, likened to the Good Samaritan by this sophisticated man of the cloth—this is high praise! "Jim Gritter...good Samaritan." My goodness, Father Tom sure knows how to turn a phrase.

It is also the craziest thing anyone has ever said about me.

You will recall that Jesus tells the story of the Good Samaritan to help us understand what it means to be a good neighbor. It is one of the most famous parables in the Bible, and it has always made me squirm. A traveler has been accosted by bandits and left in the road in rough condition. In quick succession, a couple of upright religious figures encounter the crime scene and deftly pass on the other side of the street. At last a religious nobody comes along, and promptly attends to the needs of the wounded stranger. The care is immediate, comprehensive, generous, and unconditional.

Father Tom was correct to place me in this archetypical story of hospitality. I've been aware of this disturbing parable all my life, and I have always known it was about me. More precisely, I have always known that I was one of the stiffs hightailing it to the other side of the street. I mean, what was that Samaritan thinking to get involved in a train wreck like that—bloody, inconvenient, rife with potential legal entanglements and cross-cultural complications, and expensive to boot? I'm wired like those bright religious fellows; I know how they operate. The trick is to keep one's nose in a book and claim oblivion when strange things happen. I'm sure that when they got to the office and heard about the incident in conversation around the water cooler, they were shocked. "When did you say it happened? Man, I must have just missed it because I went through that neighborhood right about that time. Didn't see a thing. Goodness, that could have been me! That's really frightening. Makes me crazy that the politicians are always talking about crime, but never do a darn thing about it."

I tell this story of Father Tom's preposterous comment because I want to confess early on that this hospitality thing is a struggle for me. Like many of you, I have a lot to learn about it. Every tactic to dodge its responsibilities tempts me, often successfully. You are not reading the thoughts of a hospitality expert; you are joining a novice's good-faith effort to get better at something important. I tell the story because I think it offers hope. After all, there is a chance that Father Tom is partially correct. Maybe there are times when, against the grain of my reflexive avoidance, I don't cross the street. Maybe I have ministered to a few birthparents and adoptive persons lying crumpled beside the road, and maybe now and then I have taken down the number of the steamrollers that flattened them. Here's the point: If a chicken like me can override the impulse to avoid the stranger in distress, maybe you can too.

With that confession out of the way, let's get rolling with a wholehearted welcome to this discussion of hospitality. How could a book featuring hospitality start without a welcome? So, welcome! Welcome to the world of adoptive hospitality. This book offers a perspective unlike others you have encountered, so it is an act of trust for you to consider this point of view. I appreciate that trust and sincerely hope it is rewarded.

A hospitable approach to this life-altering experience holds, in my opinion, great promise, but I am not naïve about this. Not for a minute do I think that hospitality is the answer to all of the challenges associated with adoption. I know that many people considering adoption—adoptive parents and birthparents alike—will not be attracted to the hospitable way. Many of these folks are in a hurry, and I understand that it is not easy to practice hospitality when it feels like time's a-wasting. I know, too, that it is very difficult to attend to the needs of others when one's own needs cry out for relief. Others, clinging to what Thomas Merton called "the illusion of autonomy" (Merton & Bochen, 1997, p. 72), are too suspicious or frightened to get involved with others. When the action turns a little sketchy or complicated, they immediately cross over to the other side of the street.

For others peering into the world of adoption, hospitality will be a great find. They may be a little wary at the outset, but I believe they will be pleased when it dawns on them that adoption done well is really about simple decency. With so much of the contemporary adoption scene hinging on money, glitz, and cleverness, there is something refreshing about an approach rooted in simple grace and respect. They will discover that hospitality is a gateway to adoption at its best.

Hospitality provides a way to work with one of adoption's most uncomfortable realities—the inequality of power that participants hold as they enter the experience. There are exceptions, but the typical adoption brings people together from markedly different circumstances: one advantaged, the other disadvantaged. Unless this dynamic is somehow mitigated, adoption teeters on the edge of exploitation. Hospitality does not gloss over this bleak prospect. To the contrary, it recognizes that social power and capacity matter more than we would like to admit, and it offers a way to lessen this tension. Granted, there are clumsy, patronizing versions of hospitality that exacerbate these differences, but in its better forms, hospitality has a way of cutting through differences so we discover our shared humanity. With layers of advantage and disadvantage peeled away, the resulting encounter is intensely personal. Those who hang tough may discover that everyone is more vulnerable than they admitted early on, yet stronger too. When the power associated with advantage and disadvantage is shed and shared, we stand a chance to be good to each other in ways we had never imagined.

The lens of hospitality brings other issues into sharper focus, too. It helps us understand how it all gets rolling, how adoptive participants move from uneasy strangers in the early phases to compatriots traveling a shared path for the long haul. Just as importantly, an understanding of the roles of guest and host highlights the liveliness of adoptive relationships. This is no small thing, for try as we might to stay conscious of the dynamism of these relationships, we easily regress into thinking that adoption is a point-in-time event. It is not easy to remain mindful of the vibrant quality of adoption when we hit those placid stretches when it seems that nothing special is happening. If the hospitable approach drives home the fact that adoptions are alive and ever-evolving, it will be an important contribution.

The hospitable liveliness of adoption becomes clear as we watch the children move from infancy to emancipation. Ordinarily we describe that developmental journey in terms of autonomy or differentiation. From the perspective of guest-host dynamics, however, we see the children in a new light. The hospitality-based view of adoption suggests we view them as *emerging hosts*. As these youngsters grow in understanding of their circumstances and in their overall competence, their influence naturally swells. Incrementally, they assume greater responsibility for their various relationships. In the end, they will determine whom they welcome and who, if anyone, is held at arm's length. This is an exciting way to think about the adoptive experience because it projects the child as a full-fledged participant in her or his life story, a significant departure from the passivity that has been foisted on them for so long. Seen through the lens of hospitality, adoption is not something that happened to a child at some point in the past. Rather, it is an ongoing experience.

To help us stay mindful of this shift from passivity to activity, I refer to the children of adoption as *adoptive* rather than as *adopted*.

The modern practice of open adoption is well into its third decade, and people are eager to gauge its effectiveness. But what do we mean by success? How do we measure this movement? Some of the early research has examined the satisfaction of adoptive parents and birth-parents with their arrangements. As the children of openness get older, their appraisal of the experience will be rightly coveted. Their impressions are of great importance, but how will they reach their conclusions? What brings them satisfaction and what leaves them frustrated? Whether or not they are conscious of it, I believe they will be commenting on the extent of the hospitality involved. Did we work with each other? Were we respectful? Did we mess with each other, or were we affirming and helpful? Did we find ways to honor our differences? If, as my psychologist friend Dr. Randolph Severson suggests, adoption is essentially a spiritual experience, then these questions that probe the quality of the relationships will be at least as useful as questions that tackle easier-to-measure variables like the form and quantity of communication.

No doubt we have been more fixated on the amount of interaction than we need to be. We were quite prescriptive in our early years of open adoption practice and eager to organize adoptions featuring maximum contact between the participants. As we had no precedent to outline the norms of open adoption, we presumed that the more contact there was, the better the outcome. It is not that simple. With the benefit of experience, we know it does not always work that way. As I reflect on how the adoptions we helped organize have played out, I confess that contact between birth- and adoptive families is less frequent than we expected. More eye-opening, though, is the quality of many of these relationships. Where shame once prevailed, we now see affirmation. These adoptive relationships are meaningful, enduring, and healthy. I have attended enough funerals of open adoption participants to know that these families are there for each other in times of need. Also, I am delighted with the unforeseen connections we have enabled. None of us anticipated in those early years that friendships would develop between birth-grandmothers and adoptive grandmothers, or that adoptive fathers would emerge as father figures to children remaining with their birth-families. The amount of contact between families may be less than we envisioned, but the breadth and depth of their interaction is greater than we ever imagined.

The perspective of hospitality helps me understand this outcome. The rub is found in our early prescriptive thinking, a mode of operation that is at odds with hospitality. Striving to accept others as they are, hospitality seldom concocts a script for appropriate behavior. Rather, it strives to create a context in which remarkable things can happen. As adoption professionals, as hosts to a cast of bruised and vulnerable strangers, we bring people together and set them up for rewarding relationships. It will always be up to them, though, to breathe life into these connections. The relationship is theirs, not ours, and that is as it should be. Don't get me wrong—frequency of contact is important—but I must admit, in the long run, that the quality of attitudes is far more crucial than the rate of contact.

One more thing about hospitality: It defends us from the siren call of selfishness. Given the critical sense of need that most participants feel as they enter the adoptive experience, it is easy for them to don blinders and ignore the similarly urgent needs of the others involved. It is tempting to play the game slyly, giving occasional lip service to the interests of others, but all the while doggedly advancing one's agenda with only incidental regard for anyone else. This approach is easily justified, but thank goodness, most of us feel uneasy about benefiting from someone else's disaster without taking his or her interests into account. Hospitality puts "the other" back on the radar screen and helps us be the sort of people we prefer to be. Hospitality offers an ethic of engagement, a pleasing alternative to societal trends that celebrate excessive independence. In the words of Father Daniel Homan and Lonni Collins Pratt, "Hospitality is a lively, courageous, and convivial way of living that challenges our compulsion either to turn away or to turn inward and disconnect ourselves from others" (2002, p. 9).

As inviting as the hospitable approach to adoption may be, it is not an easy path for anyone to follow. There are complicating factors to consider. To fully come to terms with hospitality we need to work through its uneasy interaction with another appealing concept: namely, privacy. We need to understand the limits of hospitality and give thought to boundary setting. And, given the austere and competitive realities that service providers contend with—realities that place a great premium on efficiency—we need to explore ways that agencies can justify and "make room" for hospitality-driven procedures.

Over the course of my work in adoption I have been involved with two great struggles. The first grappling was with secrecy. We countered that stifling mindset by promoting candor, and it is evident that openness increasingly carries the day. The second challenge, the commercialization of adoption, is more difficult to resist because it fits so well into the free market spirit of the day. The world of commerce has much to teach, but we do well to bear in mind writer Os Guiness' observation that "The sign of a good society is the level and number of things acknowledged to be beyond market values" (1998, p. 137). When adoption is reduced to advertising, frilly resumés, and contract negotiations, and money looms large, what are children but a commodity? In the marketplace that adoption has become, the goal of finding homes for children has given way to the task of finding children for adults. This transition is taking place with astonishingly little protest from the field, and so far the hearty few sounding the alarm have offered little by way of remedy.

I propose we check this gathering force with a generous dose of hospitality. It seems so little, yet this mustard seed needs planting. A modest, almost pitiful counter thrust, it brings to mind an observation of the philosopher William James. Regarding the underestimated power of the small act, he wrote:

> I am done with great things and big things, great institutions and big success; and am for those tiny, invisible molecular moral forces that work from individual to

individual through the crannies of the world, like so many rootlets, or like the capillary oozing of water, yet which, if you give them time, will rend the hardest moments of man's pride. (James, 1926, p. 90)

Or as Mother Teresa famously said, "We can do no great things—only small things, with great love" (*Love*, 2007, pp. 72–73). Her words direct us to the hospitable path. If we wish to make a difference in any endeavor, including adoption, we will respond to those around us with small acts of courageous respect. Hospitality is the way forward.

TOWARD HOSPITABLE ADOPTION LANGUAGE

Hospitality offers a practical and pleasing way of thinking and talking about adoption. This is more important than it sounds because we have struggled in this field to find language that works. Sometimes it is syrupy and drips with euphemisms, other times it is stuffy and loaded with jargon. More and more it seems—even though we are making plans for children—we speak the calculated language of commerce. None of these approaches strikes a satisfactory tone; each misses the mark in some important ways. The language of hospitality, however, works on several levels. It speaks to heart, soul, and mind; it's capable of stirring our spirit, yet down-to-earth and understandable. It is useful in helping us comprehend a dynamic process, and it invites an attitude of respect. This is language that suits the sensitivity and complexity of the experience. I hope it puts words to a melody that welcoming families and practitioners have been humming for years.

As we dig deeper into the subject of hospitality, I intend to breathe new life into some words that have expired before their time. Somewhere between 1944 and 1965, the gap between the second edition of Webster's International Dictionary and the third, we lost a few words having to do with hospitality. Since their loss depletes a language set already too spare, I propose we exhume them. Consider a few of these troopers who are at risk or who have already crossed over as they have been defined in 1944's second edition. *Hospitious*, for example. Although it does not add anything to *hospitable*, it gives that hardworking word a rest and is less likely to bring a sprawling medical building to mind. Moreover, I confess that I like the way it sounds. And how did we let a sturdy word like *hospitator*, designating "a giver or receiver of hospitality," slip away? Who

9

among us can resist the lure of becoming a hospitator? I'd like to dust off the antique jewel *hospitate* because it is hospitality in verb form. Since there are no modern verb forms for hospitality, it is difficult to speak of its doing. When we attempt to put hospitality into play, we are stuck with the bland verbs *offer* and *receive*. Committed hospitators deserve better. In this "bowling alone" era, we need these words of connection more than ever. With your indulgence, then, we will dust off these old-timers and put them to work again as we explore the junction of adoption and hospitality.

Hospitality flavors the language of adoption in three important ways. First, a premium is placed on clarity and accuracy because, in the anxious undertaking of adoption, each participant needs to know exactly where she fits in and what sort of challenges and responsibilities she is taking on. Hospitable language is often "down home" and unpretentious; picturesque simplicity is preferred to euphemisms or jargon. Severson writes of "right words" which, "when you find them, when the soul shines through, even the simplest phrase or some fleeting expression compresses into it a whole universe of previously felt but inarticulate meaning" (1998, p. xvii). Hospitable language welcomes words of that caliber. Second, hospitable language seeks to convey the dynamism of adoptive relationships. It is inclusive and action-oriented. Ever on the lookout for shifts in the guest-host dynamic, subtle or dramatic, it searches for expressions that convey nuances of relatedness. Third, respectful discourse strives to create and preserve ample room for participants to be themselves. It relishes roomy words and phrases while it guards against pressure and presumption. In particular, hospitious speakers are interested in using words that make room for the child to find and use her emerging voice.

Words That Are Accurate

Is it better to speak of *adoptees* or *adopted persons*? Consensus has yet to emerge, but at least one opinion leader has settled it in her mind. Dr. Joyce Maguire Pavao has come out on the side of "adopted person." She puts it this way: "'Adopted person' is better. 'Adoptee' is another way of demeaning that person. It's a belittling term" (Pavao, Interview 2004). If *adoptee* demeans, belittles, or sets people apart or if at least some people hear it that way, we can do without the term. Perhaps there is another alternative; namely, "adoptive person," the term favored in this book. The difference is more suggestive than denotative. The suffix -*ive* signals that effort or action is involved while -*ed* often indicates past tense. A way to see how they play out is to apply them to "adapt," a word that is both relevant and similar in sound. "Adaptive" intimates an ongoing capacity while "adapted" suggests a past accommodation. The distinction is admittedly fine, but any bit of language that nudges us in the direction of acknowledging the ongoing activity of the child, the emerging host, merits consideration.

Children have an uncanny ability to invent expressions that amiably distinguish the important people they relate to. A youngster comes to mind who, between his birth and adoptive clans, had nine grandparents actively involved in his life. For him the statement "We're going to Grandma's house" was inadequate because it only narrowed the field to five destinations. Needing language that supplied more information, this lad, who had earlier settled on "Papa Louie" as the title for his birthfather, dubbed his paternal birthgrandmother "Grandma Louie." Not all children are as clever, so there are times when we need to help them find workable language.

Words That Are Relational

Almost everyone involved in adoption is sensitive to the possessive pronouns scattered through our conversations. These potent little words serve an important purpose as they help us sort out relationships between people. When it comes to adoption, though, sorting is tricky business.

Pronouns both *profess* and *possess*. Sometimes we use possessive pronouns to declare relatedness, and other times we use them to claim ownership. Meaning often hinges on intonation. The way I say, "This is *my* child," for example, makes a great difference. Am I declaring pride in this goofy kid, or am I warning you to stay away? Most of the trouble with possessive pronouns resides in their potential to imply exclusivity. When I declare that something is mine, it is reasonable for you to conclude that I am telling you that it is not yours. There is hazard, then, that our efforts to lovingly identify with and claim loved ones will be understood as declarations of exclusivity and ownership. Fortunately, relief is available in the form of plural pronouns, and hospitality-minded participants make generous use of them. This child is neither *yours* nor *mine*; she is first and foremost her *own* unique person, but beyond that, she is *ours* to exalt in. Since healthy claiming is reciprocal, another way to handle this is to change the reference point. Instead of declaring, "She is my daughter," I might proudly state, "I am her father. I belong to her." The concept of belonging is a promising antidote to possession. Dr. Pavao, herself an adoptive person, states it well. "Belonging is a wonderful way to not be possessed, but to be joined" (Pavao, Interview 2004).

Words That Make Room

A hallmark of hospitality is that it makes room for people to find their way. It is careful not to crowd or pressure them. A commitment to hospitious adoption means we will be vigilant for words or expressions that in any way crowd or corner those who are journeying through the experience. One common version of pressure is presumption. For example, many of us refer to the pregnant woman or couple who are considering the possibility of entrusting their children to adoptive parents as *birthparents*. It may seem like splitting hairs to some, but I believe it is very important that we not cast them as birthparents until they have actually taken the legal step of entrusting their child to the adoptive family. The premature use of the word *birthparent* implies that things are more settled than they actually are, and it fuels the fires of presumption. Even if it is cumbersome, we do well to find language that grants them whatever wiggle room they may need to change course if need be. If we discipline ourselves to speak of *potential birthparents* or *prospective birthparents* or better yet, *the couple that is considering adoption*, we offer them the space they deserve and at the same time remind ourselves to take nothing for granted.

A couple more examples of presumptive language come to mind. Some observers call a potential birthparent's change of heart about adoption a *reversal*. That is more of a word than the situation requires. When we refer to someone changing her mind in everyday language, we do not speak of reversals. We simply say, "She changed her mind." That happens routinely in day-to-day circumstances, and it sometimes happens in the adoption realm, too.

I have long been uncomfortable with the phrase "make an adoption plan." For starters, *make* is a tepid verb that would surely draw the attention of any conscientious editor. Her red ink swiftly changes "Brianne is making an adoption plan" to "Brianne is planning an adoption." More critically, we sometimes make too much of the word *plan*. There are times when the plan of potential birthparents is viewed more as a solemn commitment than as a rough draft. Perhaps it is best to simply say, "Brianne is considering adoption."

Words That Invite Participation

The defining word in this field is *adopt*. Meaning to take in as one's own, it works well to describe the action of the family that is welcoming and incorporating a child as a full-fledged family member. Clearly, though, *adopt* works less well for the other participants. When birthparents try to use it, they uncomfortably contort it into *adopted out*. Adoptive persons exist as the object of the verb, not its subject. For them, it necessarily takes the passive form; they say "I was adopted." The point is, one verb does not fit all. Everyone deserves a verb of their own. In the vernacular of elementary school teachers, each participant can benefit from a "working word" that uniquely fits her activity.

The word that best suits the action of the birthfamily in open adoption is *entrust*. To entrust is to invest with a trust; to commission;

to give for safekeeping; to have faith in and place hope in; or to rely on someone's character, ability, strength, and honesty. While the word does not work for birthparents whose rights are terminated against their wishes, *entrust* fits perfectly for those who actively arrange for another family to stand in their place. First, it is an action word, muscular and observable. Second, it draws appropriate attention to the primary birthparent task; namely, granting trust and commissioning others to take on the responsibilities of active duty parenting. Best of all, it works for those who live it. I have seen birthparents light up at the word. "Yes!" they say, "that's it! That fits. That's exactly what I have in mind." It spares them the wilting terminology of the battlefield—*surrender, give up, relinquish,* and *abandon*—though there are no doubt times when it must feel like those terms apply. In an age of expanding birthparent involvement, *entrust* conveys at least a measure of their sleeves-rolled-up love and concern.

So what is the verb for the children of adoption? At the moment, there is no obvious answer. It has only lately occurred to us to welcome them as active participants, and we have not yet found adequate language for their actions. Hospitious possibilities exist and merit exploration, though I believe this is a question for the community of adoptive persons to settle. *Integrate* deserves consideration because it describes the emotional and psychological work adoptive persons do as they craft a sense of identity. They have their work cut out for them as they weave the past and present into a coherent future. Perhaps *manage* will emerge as their verb, for they have several relationships to juggle as they move toward greater ownership of their story. Maybe these heretofore verbless souls will *acknowledge, accept,* and *affirm* the various people who have contributed to their stories. In the end, we may make an interesting discovery: We may find that the adoptive person is the ultimate adopter. As an adult, she will decide whom she welcomes and takes in as her own. We may even discover that in the best of circumstances, all of the participants end up *adopting* each other, incorporating all of the others into their lives.

The language of adoption merits continuous discussion. Lists and charts and chapters may help for a season, but they are soon obsolete. Our search for better words is relentless. Given the dynamism of healthy adoptions, we need language that is alive and adaptive. If we envision adoption as an amiable, ongoing effort to meet the emerging needs of children, our words need to dance with life, truth, and hospitality.

CHAPTER 1

OLD DOGS AND FARMERS:
Hospitality as the Gateway to Connection

When Philip and Denise Peters first showed up for their orientation meeting, I was a little uneasy about their prospects. They were a plainspoken farm family, a bit on the heavyset side, and I was concerned that life on the farm might not draw much interest from the birthparent realm. Happily, my reservations disappeared in our subsequent intake session when Philip made an offhand comment that pierced my prejudicial thinking. "I don't know who you're going to take into this program," he began, "but I do know this: If you're an old dog wandering the roads with no place to call home, you'd be a smart old dog if you turned up the Peterses' driveway."

Although I could not put a word to it at the time, I knew immediately that Philip had touched on something essential. For a long time I understood this quality in terms of "good-heartedness." That characterization still holds, but now, with the benefit of some time to ponder that comment, I realize that he was describing the spirit of hospitality. With a few simple words, he captured the essence of adoption. Philip Peters understands that when all is said and done, adoption at its best is about welcoming others and making room for them in our hearts and in our lives.

Adoption is about hospitality. The case for this observation can be made with one simple question. What everyday expression do we use to describe hospitable folks? Of them we say, "They make you feel at home." Let those words sink in for a moment. Can you think of a better way to describe the purpose of adoption? Is there anything sweeter than feeling at home? Is not our most fervent wish for our children that they feel at home?

If hospitality is at the heart of adoption, we need to understand it better. To be sure, we are not talking about garden parties and polite small talk. And there is another important distinction we need to make early on. There is a hospitality look-alike that is actually its inverse. Theologian Christine Pohl describes this counterfeit with great clarity. In her superb exploration of hospitality, *Making Room*, she notes,

> There is a kind of hospitality that keeps people needy strangers while fostering an illusion of relationship and connection. It both disempowers and domesticates guests while it reinforces the hosts' power, control, and sense of generosity. It is profoundly destructive to the people it welcomes. It is the kind of help which, in Philip Hallie's words, "fills their hands but breaks their hearts." (1999, p. 120)

Pohl rightly warns us that this can be tricky territory; we can inflict damage in the name of hospitality. The distinction between effective and ineffective hospitality is mostly attitudinal. It is the difference between a respectful attitude that says "We're in this together" and a spirit of condescension that accentuates our differences and diminishes everyone involved.

I think of hospitality as an extension of grace from one party to another, an elemental willingness to reach out to others with goodwill and respect in the effort to create a larger "we." It is going beyond the ordinary to open our lives to others and to make room for them. In the words of writer Amy Oden,

> ...Hospitality is not so much a singular act of welcome as it is a way, an orientation that attends to otherness, listening and learning, valuing and honoring. The hospitable one looks for God's redemptive presence in the other, confident it is there, if one only has eyes to see and ears to hear. (2001, pp. 14–15)

Join me in a swift overview of this "way" of being known as hospitality. We have just stated that it is rooted in an orientation of readiness and openness. Readiness leads to the simple act of noticing. Noticing seems a small thing, but it matters greatly. The temptation to ignore those who strike us as different is great, for we know from experience that things are usually simpler when we look the other way. With enough practice, we become accomplished at maintaining our oblivion. I am always amazed when I walk through a big city to notice how determined people are to avoid eye contact. Torrents of people stream by, but few if any are inclined to acknowledge my existence. Adoption sometimes seems like crowded, scary territory, too, and it is not uncommon for people to move through the process with this same practiced oblivion.

Noticing affirms, but it also complicates things. Once the needfulness of another is noticed, once a plaintive face comes into focus, the awkward question of whether or not to get involved is posed. Against the grain of modern instinct, hospitable people choose to get involved. Getting involved is personal. It means actually doing something. For someone like me who would rather *talk* about doing something, this is challenging. It means my body is involved; I have to make eye contact and worry about my footwork. I move stuff around and risk a sore back. But then I receive a glass of cool water and offer one to my neighbor. It also means my spirit is engaged, not detached or indifferent. Forget about tidiness, efficiency, and predictability. Importantly, I am not responding to a problem or a situation; I am one person responding to another. On some level, conscious or unconscious, it occurs to me that our roles could easily be switched. Have I been in the wrong place at the wrong time? Have I been offensive? Alien? Unlucky? Have I been the awkward, out-of-sync stranger?

Hospitality rolls up its sleeves and gets involved, but it is careful not to *mess* with people. It accepts them and values them as they are. Beloved spiritual writer Henri Nouwen wrote,

> The paradox of hospitality is that it wants to create emptiness, not a fearful emptiness, but a friendly emptiness

where strangers can enter and discover themselves as created free; free to sing their own songs, speak their own lan-
guages, dance their own dances; free also to leave and
follow their own vocations. Hospitality is not a subtle
invitation to adopt the life style of the host, but the gift
of a chance for the guest to find his own. (1975, p. 51)

So hospitality is about trust and respect. Often we view respect
as a sort of deference paid to the high and mighty. That is "special
occasion respect." Hospitious respect does not go overboard with deference because, to the extent that it signals that we hold unequal
status, it divides us. Truly hospitable people do not treat us like we
are special; they treat us like we belong. It's refrigerator privileges
and the blunt expectation that we will pick up after ourselves. Their
treatment tells me I am no better than anyone else, *and I am no worse
than anyone else, either.*

Hospitality affects everyone involved with adoption. No matter
our role, each will be a stranger, and each will also have the opportunity to greet a stranger. Each will be guest, and each will be host.
Along the way we will know moments of needfulness as well
as moments of advantage; some of the time an old dog, some of
the time a farmer.

One of the ways the early church fathers thought of hospitality
was "safeguarding the pilgrim." This is a useful perspective in adoption—surely a pilgrimage of sorts—for we all bear responsibility for
the well-being of the others involved as together we meander
through unfamiliar terrain. Recently I read a story in which
Robert Benne, a Lutheran seminary professor, reports on the
decision-making process he and his wife went through when they
discovered they were pregnant at age 40 with three kids already on
board, the youngest age 9. Speaking of their resolution with grace-
filled warmth, Benne writes, "I am so grateful for the steadfast
Christian hospitality of my wife, who was willing to accept the most
vulnerable of strangers. She carried me along. And we are delighted
to have a 20-year-old son who is now in his third year of college"
(1998, p. 32). His comment points us to the place where hospitality

begins, the hospitality a mother extends to the mysterious, inconvenient child raising Cain in her belly. The child's pilgrimage
through the maze of adoption starts with his first mother's bold act
of hospitality and is later sustained by the hospitality of the adoptive parents. "Welcome," each set of parents says to the bug-eyed
newcomer, "welcome."

The next needful strangers are the would-be adoptive parents.
Often they do not look very needful, but they are, some to the point
of desperation. In many ways their lives are moving forward, but in
this one crucial and tender dimension, fertility, they have been
derailed. Their situation necessitates that they catch the attention
of a woman or couple grappling with an untimely pregnancy. To the
chagrin of some, they are left courting the favor of a population they
might not otherwise notice and acknowledge.

For a brief season potential birthparents play host to potential
adoptive parents. While would-be adoptive parents are usually
keenly aware of the power the pregnant family holds, for a variety of
reasons many expectant parents are not aware that they occupy the
advantaged position. Often they are not socially powerful in the first
place, and their stressful circumstance has them more off-balance
than ever. They may be too distressed to notice that the others
involved are, at least for that moment, even more needful. If that
were not enough, it is not uncommon for the service provider to
usurp their power by slipping into the role of host and acting as if
he holds the cards.

For potential birthparents, the time of hosting swiftly slips away.
Once they officially pass the torch of parental responsibility to the
adoptive parents, the hospitality roles are inverted for the long haul.
The adoptive parents become the advantaged hosts, and the birthparents become the dependent guests.

The shift of permanent authority between the families is a critical juncture that tests their capacity to provide and receive hospitality. If the transition is not handled well, birthparents are at risk
to go through the adoption experience as perpetual supplicants. This
is a startling prospect. One might suppose that adoptive parents

would offer reciprocal hospitality as a matter of course once they have been officially installed as the legal parents. After all, they are no longer strangers to each other. What is more, the original hosts have blessed them in an incomparable manner. Sadly, though, these factors do not always translate into reciprocal hospitality. It turns out that the birthfamilies still seem scary to the newly installed parents, possibly scarier than ever now that they have something wonderful—a child—to lose. Birthparents strike them as big-time candidates for regret. As Jana Wolff put it in the first edition of *Secret Thoughts of an Adoptive Mother*, "What will happen once you figure out what you've done?" (1997, p. 17) Birthparents start to loom in their imagination as likely rivals for this extraordinary child's affection. "Maybe," the new parents start to think, "it would be safer to send them packing. Maybe we have gotten carried away with this open adoption stuff and should calm down a little. Maybe it would be better for everyone if we took a couple of steps back." It is never difficult to find reasons to avoid hospitality.

So we have seen that adoptive hospitality begins with the welcome the birthmother extends first to the child and next to the prospective adoptive parents. Then, as the power shifts, the roles are inverted. Adoptive parents move to the forefront, and the birthparents assume a complementary role. Often we act as if the story ends there, but the hospitious perspective suggests the dynamism of the relationships continue. At some point, advancing in years and in personal responsibility, the adoptive young person grows into the role of host to both sets of parents. Surely this ultimate hospitality shift will be the most interesting and significant of all. Calling their own shots at last, adoptive adults will likely find their status as belated host a challenging mixture of liberation and burden.

I don't know about you, but I can't get that old wandering dog out of my mind. My heart goes out to that needful creature. An old codger like that is not good for much. He is not going to scare off any intruders, and he won't shine at a game of fetch. The welcome he receives is based on something other than usefulness. We smile when we come across an old hound dozing on a porch. His oblivious slumber signals that things are right in the world, that this is a place where all creatures great or sleepy are treated with dignity—not because they are useful but simply because they exist. The old dog reminds us that a guest often brings unexpected blessings.

What does an old dog look for in his time of need? By Philip Peters's account, some old dogs are smarter than others, so let's amend the question and ask about the instincts of a *smart* old critter. A truly savvy old timer is going to look for folks for whom hospitality is second nature. For some genial souls, hospitality is automatic. Gifted with generous hearts and helpful dispositions, it is an unconscious reflex for them to set others at ease in their time of need. The right thing trumps the convenient or safe thing every time. When I told the Peterses how powerful the comment about the homeless dog was for me, they were surprised. They responded with a quizzical look that asked, "What's the fuss?" and "You don't get out too often, do you?"

The reflexive, there's-nothing-to-think-about hospitality that the Peterses offer can be found everywhere, but perhaps it is most common in the country and in the inner city. In those venues, one fully expects to spend ample time among both the needful and the helpful. It goes with the territory. Unsophisticated people who live from one unpredictable moment to the next are often more familiar with hospitality than are those who are able to buy their way out of distress. Rookie social workers prefer doing home studies with the well-heeled. Workers with more experience look forward to spending time with prospects who bear the marks of having been roughed up and softened by the give-and-take of hospitable living. More often than not, birthparents share this preference.

The naturally hospitable are the healers in our midst. Almost effortlessly, it seems, they bridge our differences and bring out our best. They have what Archbishop Desmond Tutu calls *ubuntu*.

> A person with *ubuntu* is welcoming, hospitable, warm and generous, willing to share. Such people are open, available to others, willing to be vulnerable, affirming of others, do not feel threatened that others are able and good,

for they have a proper self-assurance that comes from
knowing that they belong in a greater whole. They
know they are diminished when others are humiliated,
diminished when others are oppressed, diminished when
others are treated as if they were less than who they are.
(2004, p. 26)

For the rest of us, the *ubuntu*-challenged, hospitality is an attitude
to be cultivated and a skill to be learned. For the sake of others and
our own sake as well, we need to consciously go out of our way to
practice this ancient art.

How can we be more like the Peterses? We can begin with a few
elementary ideas. First, we can practice their generosity of spirit.
That means seeing the best in folks and giving them the benefit of
the doubt. It means downplaying their flaws and focusing instead on
their strengths. Second, we can mimic their helpful spirit. Instead of
analyzing the situation and hatching action plans, we can simply
pitch in and do what needs to be done. Third, like the Peters family, we can reject "we/they" thinking. Birthparents, adoptive parents,
adoptive persons, and service providers are all the same people,
sometimes able to help and sometimes needing help. Nobody has
rank on anyone else. We/they thinking is antithetical to the spirit
of hospitality. There may be a gap in effectiveness between birthparents and adoptive parents at the time of placement, but time has
a way of erasing and sometimes even inverting these differences.

The giving and receiving of hospitality warms and expands our
circumstances. It surrounds children with love. Why, then, don't we
see more of it?

One force that quashes hospitality is the spirit of commercialism.
When adoption is organized as a business transaction, it is intentionally impersonal. In that minimalist approach, participants are
encouraged to keep their distance. They may know something about
each other, but the process keeps them emotionally distant. They
are strangers by design. These arrangements may feature some elements of openness, but they fall far short of the hospitality standard.

Another impediment is our affection for convenience. If there is a reasonable opening in my schedule, I am generally willing to lend a hand. When I am caught up with my sundry preoccupations, however, you may be out of luck. How dare you disturb my comfort with news of your misfortune? Because my interest in preserving personal ease runs deep—I nurture it as if it were a sacred entitlement—my availability for hospitable endeavors is significantly diminished.

The greatest barrier to hospitality is fear. We avoid getting involved with others because we are afraid we might get hurt. I wonder, though, when we came up with the idea that adoption ought to be super-safe? How could it be? Is having babies safe? Is raising children safe? And, really, is playing it safe all that great, anyway? What is life like for people who play it safe all the time? In a lively, healthy way, the practice of hospitality takes us a little closer to the edge where exhilarating, meaningful life happens.

Courageous hospitality sets the stage for building deeper-than-ordinary relationships. The hope is that hospitality will grow into friendship and friendship will in turn evolve into kinship. The most satisfying adoptions follow that course, but even if that most desirable evolution does not occur, a foundation of hospitality is sufficient to sustain very cordial adoptive relationships. We are not very likely to get to the intimacy of friendship and kinship if we have not first passed through the gate of hospitality.

Is hospitality always rewarded? Hardly. Hospitality has its risks and its limitations. Some strangers are so wounded that they rebuff or mishandle the hospitable gesture. But is hospitality usually rewarded? No doubt. If someday you have a chance to travel through Northern Michigan and somehow end up a little lost, you would do well to turn up the Peterses' driveway. Are those folks comfortable in their own skins? Absolutely. Can you get a good meal there? Do they have people to turn to in a time of need? And, by the way, were they of interest to birthparents? Goodness, yes—three sets of them! Again we turn to theologian Pohl for insight. She writes, "Over and over again, I've come to see that in God's remarkable economy, as we make room for hospitality, more room becomes available to us for life, hope, and grace" (1999, p. xiii).

It is easy to underestimate the importance of hospitality. Keep birthparents in mind as we consider one last summarizing comment from Pohl. She observes,

> People view hospitality as quaint and tame partly because they do not understand the power of recognition. When a person who is not valued by society is received by a socially respected person or group as a human being with dignity and worth, small transformations occur... Because such actions are countercultural, they are a witness to the larger community, which is then challenged to reassess its standards and methods of valuing. Many persons who are not valued by the larger community are essentially invisible to it. Hospitality can begin a journey toward visibility and respect. (1999, p. 62)

In a low-key, inoffensive manner, hospitality challenges the accepted social order. In the small gesture of hospitality resides the germ of revolution. The fact that its power is unrecognized makes it all the more subversive. Few of us are inclined to storm the barricades of social convention, but many of us will delight in the prospect of shaking up the status quo with the genial power of hospitality.

CHAPTER 2

THE ETHIC OF HOSPITALITY:
"Strange and Amazing Things Can Happen"

There is simple beauty to hospitality. Without a lot of explanation, most of us are aware of its sweetness. We have experienced the startling, deep welcome of hospitality and reveled in the bracing sensation that even in a lonely moment we matter to someone who hardly knows us. Given that enduring memory of hospitable acceptance, it is tempting to simply declare it a self-apparent good and say no more, for the study of it risks its diminishment. The strangeness of it, though, the near-novel feel, suggests that it is far less familiar than we prefer. Good, then, to make an effort to grasp it more fully. Perhaps, if we understand the basics of hospitality better, we will offer more of it.

When we are talking about hospitality, we are talking about ethics. Philosopher Jacques Derrida put the connection between ethics and hospitality in the strongest terms. He wrote,

> One cannot speak of cultivating an ethic of hospitality. Hospitality is culture itself and not simply one ethic amongst others. Insofar as it has to do with the *ethos*, that is, the residence, one's home, the familiar place of dwelling, inasmuch as it is a manner of being there, the manner in which we relate to ourselves and to others, to others as our own or as foreigners, *ethics is hospitality*; ethics is so thoroughly coextensive with the experience of hospitality. (2001, pp. 16–17)

Conscious of it or not, like it or not, adoption's participants are interdependent and connected. One cannot be an adoptive child or adoptive parent or birthparent apart from the contributions of the others. These connections define fundamental aspects of each person's identity. That irrefutable and enduring linkage means these parties have to come to terms with who they are to each other and how they will treat one another. Ethics are in play, and circumstances require that they determine the extent of the hospitality they are willing to offer and receive.

Because open adoption is not universally embraced, we may reasonably conclude that some hold that the high road in adoption is that of disengagement. They believe, apparently, that the parties to adoption have little of value to offer each other and that it is best for them to have nothing to do with each other.

Proponents of openness are puzzled by this pessimistic ethic. Where is the morality, we wonder, in steering clear of others when we are capable of bringing a measure of relief to their concerns and needs? Preferring an ethic of engagement, we think these skeptics underestimate the capacity of adoptive participants to minister to each other and overestimate the prospect for destructive interaction. As we see it, birthparents, adoptive parents, and adoptive persons are uniquely positioned to share invigorating gifts of information, affirmation, and connection. Granted, it takes effort to interact hospitably, lots of it, but that is hardly an argument against it as a moral course. The ethical path is seldom easy. Besides—ask any parent—effort and inconvenience go with the territory whenever we set out to serve children.

Hospitality can be described as a set of attitudes and as a set of skills. We will consider three of each. More could be included, but it is important that the simplicity of hospitality shines through our discussion. These basics are enough to organize and enrich our thinking. Hospitality is founded on the attitudes of *goodwill*, *respect*, and *courage*, and it is brought to life through the skills of *noticing*, *listening*, and *creating space*. As our exploration of the subject moves forward, it will be evident that these attitudes and skills are closely related and complementary.

Goodwill

Hospitality starts with an attitude of goodwill. Since everyone operates with some measure of goodwill, this seems a promising beginning. The goodwill required to energize adoption, though, is not the tepid version that vaguely hopes things turn out okay. We are talking about visceral goodwill, a bent of the spirit and flesh that assumes the stranger in his many guises—not just the appealing or promising variations—is most likely interesting and well-intentioned. While not reckless with optimism, the person of substantial goodwill is inclined to give the stranger a chance to prove himself. She has the ability to peel back a few crusty exterior layers and discover impressive qualities at his core. She matter-of-factly notes, "Once you get past the awkwardness, addiction, poor hygiene, foul language, or any of a thousand other off-putting characteristics, you find an amazingly bright and warm person." Goodwill prompts her to scan for positive qualities in the other, not for flaws.

Goodwill identifies with the other. It does not go so far as to suggest we are the same, but it does assert that we are not so different as appearances may suggest. Despite our differences, some of which may be conspicuous, we invariably overlap in important ways, and that common ground provides opportunities for relationship building. In Tutu's words, "Those with eyes to see will know that these are brothers and sisters created by the same God and living as mutual guests in the same house provided by the same divine host" (2004, p. 52). The person of goodwill knows that roles are more fragile than they appear. That is to say, apart from some quirks of biology and luck, birthparents and adoptive parents could easily change places. Even in those instances where little common ground can be found, participants are vitally linked by their shared adoptive experience. They have some important people in common, most notably a child who looks to them to make sense of an existentially provocative circumstance.

Not only does an attitude of goodwill take a positive view of the stranger and recognize commonality, it also actively wishes the other well. Persons of goodwill are not interested in boosting their status by demoting anyone else. To the contrary, they feel diminished if the other is impugned, especially if they were somehow responsible. Agents of goodwill realize that everyone is well-served when the cause of the other is promoted. One down-to-earth adoptive father put it this way: "Our daughter will love us all the more for including her birthmother and always speaking well of her."

A useful way to flesh out our understanding of goodwill is to consider its inverse. The opposite of goodwill is prejudice. Because prejudice presumes without evidence that the stranger is worrisome and a poor candidate for trust, it runs counter to the spirit of hospitality. If we find ourselves hesitant to offer hospitality, we do well to search our souls for evidence of prejudice.

Respect

Pointing out that adoptive participants are interdependent does not mean they are equals. In fact, the reality of adoption presumes one family, at least at the time an adoption is contemplated, is more situated than the other. After all, if adoptive families did not constitute some form of progress for the child, there would be no reason to alter her life course. This initial inequality means they will need to find ways to work out their differences. Some differences are appealing, but others confound and complicate. In *Respect in a World of Inequality*, Richard Sennett writes,

> It takes a long time, and a great deal of trust, for highly educated professionals and unskilled laborers to speak freely to one another; the beautiful and the ugly don't talk easily to each other about their bodies; people whose lives are full of adventure have trouble 'relating' to the experience of people constrained within narrow routines. (2003, p. 22)

We might add the fertile and infertile as well as commissioned and decommissioned parents to the list of the uncomfortably coupled.

We can respect someone simply for existing, for being human, but our positive regard means more when it reflects a genuine feeling that the person is worthy of respect. There is much to admire about adoption's participants. There are, of course, individuals who move through the experience with a scorched-earth policy, but they are the exception. People close to adoption marvel at the courage of birthparents whose decisions run counter to prevailing social pressures. We also marvel at the generosity of spirit shown by adoptive parents who rebuff the temptations of convenience and open their homes and hearts not only to a child, but also to the cast of characters who love that child. It is not difficult to respect those who stand steadfastly by their beliefs, especially when their convictions are carried out at high personal cost.

There may be attitudes that can be faked, but respect is not one of them. It makes no sense to speak of half-hearted or lukewarm respect, for any diminution of it effectively cancels it. Among those who are sensitive to the issue of respect because they have experienced little of it, the slightest hesitancy or equivocation is taken as disrespect. A flicker of pity, condescension, or insincerity can undermine months of constructive interaction.

Courage

A spirit of goodwill and respect keeps open the door of opportunity, but something more is required if we are to walk through it. Clearly, that something is courage. Hospitality is, after all, risky business, and it takes courage to set it in motion. It is a calling that enables the innately brave to shine, but where do the rest of us find this strength?

Sometimes we find it in the example of others. We see them standing tall and are inspired do the same. Or we witness some form of injustice and, fueled with indignation, reflexively move into action. Looking back, we are not sure exactly what got into us, but we knew we could not just sit there and watch. There are times, too, when we find ourselves emboldened by our belief that we are involved with something important, that we are representing something bigger than ourselves. Perhaps we simply grow weary of always playing it safe. No doubt some find the courage to act because they are avoiding an even more fearful course. Theologian Pohl points out, "People for whom hospitality is a disposition and a habit are less afraid of the risks associated with caring for strangers than they are of the possibility of cutting themselves off from the needs of strangers" (1999, p. 176). However or wherever we find courage, we are likely more capable of it than we realize. Many of the small acts of decency we manage in daily life contain a kernel of courage.

When it comes to adoption, courage is often undone by complacency. Our fears restrain us, but so does our affection for comfort. Emotional comfort is important to us, and we zealously guard it. Our devotion to comfort, though, is not without cost, for it diminishes our willingness to get involved with the people around us. If we shy away from challenge, if we have little faith in our ability to solve problems and form meaningful connections, if we are too self-concerned to get involved, there is no prospect for hospitality.

So, these are the attitudes that underlie hospitality: goodwill, respect, and courage. Unlike their opposites—prejudice, condescension, and convenient disengagement—they set the stage for meaningful connection between strangers. These attitudes foster the behaviors of noticing, listening, and making room, skills that merit our consideration.

Noticing

Belief precedes observation; we can only see what we are willing to acknowledge. The lens of goodwill, respect, and courage broadens our vision. With this attitudinal foundation, we notice people and situations we might otherwise miss. Oden writes,

> Hospitality is characterized by a particular moral stance in the world that can best be described as readiness...Whether we are guest or host, we must be ready, ready to welcome, ready to enter another's world, ready to be vulnerable...This readiness is expectant...Such readiness takes courage, gratitude, and radical openness. (2001, p. 15)

Professor Oden is on to something. If we are not ready to encounter the stranger, we will not even notice her. She will stay embedded in the broader context, never entering into the foreground of our attention. We began this chapter by remembering a time of personal discomfort when we were unexpectedly noticed and acknowledged. Chances are we can also remember a moment when we went unnoticed. Commentator Parker Palmer writes, "An inhospitable space is one in which we feel invisible—or visible but on trial" (1997, p. 67). In adoption, we have rendered many important people invisible. Where, for example, are the birthfathers? Our eagerness to move forward with adoption makes little provision for their involvement. Even birthmothers, so central to the drama early on, too often lose their visibility once they have relinquished their rights. And when we speak knowingly of the "triad" of birthparents, adoptive parents, and adoptive children, we push siblings and grandparents to the sidelines as secondary players. Hospitious noticing recognizes that adoption invariably affects expansive networks of interested people.

Hospitality involves noticing with "eyes of the heart," as the indomitable Bishop Tutu puts it, the person who is having a hard time fitting in. He writes, "The eyes of the heart are not concerned with appearances but with essences, and as we cultivate these eyes we are able to learn from our suffering and to see the world with more loving, forgiving, humble, generous eyes" (2004, p. 72). Generous eyes, eyes that are informed by a heart of goodwill, will notice the distress of others in a way that does not think less of them for being needful. Interpersonal validation is at the heart of this generous version of noticing.

The ability to notice and get noticed matters greatly in the contemporary adoption scene as couples thinking that adoption might be the best outcome for their untimely pregnancy and families hoping to adopt try to find each other. It is a consequential endeavor, and close observers note that not all eyes are generous; some are on the lookout to take advantage of others. Seen through calculating eyes, the other, no matter how dire her circumstance, is more a candidate to provide help than to receive it. Instead of noticing a person in need, we see an opportunity to advance our purposes. This disjointed vision notices and ignores in the same glance. In this mode, the other's usefulness comes into sharp focus while her needs go unnoticed.

Listening

Listening continues the affirming attention that starts with noticing. In their helpful book *Radical Hospitality*, Homan and Pratt observe, "Listening is always involved in hospitality. The most gracious attempts we can muster are meaningless if we do not actually hear the stranger. Listening is the core of hospitality" (2002, p. 213). They go on to state,

> When a human being isn't heard, when all that is special to a child is ignored so that the child can be shaped into what the parents think the child should be—that person is in grave danger of becoming less that they were made for. …Hospitality is a way to counter the thousands of times another human being has felt less than human because others didn't listen. Listening is the power of hospitality; it is what makes hospitality the life-giving thing it is. (p. 215)

Fully attentive listening is out of the ordinary. Often we listen half-heartedly, acting as if we are tuned in when in fact our mind is somewhere else. Thomas Merton indicts us with his observation that:

> We live in a state of semi-attention to the sound of voices, music, traffic, or the generalized noise of what goes on around us all the time. This keeps us immersed in a flood of racket and words, a diffuse medium in which our consciousness is half diluted: we are not quite "thinking," not entirely responding, but we are more or less there. We are not fully present and not entirely absent; not fully withdrawn, yet not completely available. (2000, p. 74)

Ignoring undercurrents of meaning, we listen just enough to sustain superficial exchange. Sometimes we "listen" to find cues to redirect the conversation to ourselves. The whole-hearted listening of hospitality is noticeably different. It means we are fully present to the other. As Homan and Pratt point out, this presence and availability is the power of listening. Whether we are attending to close friends or strangers, we have nothing more important to offer than time and attention. What is love but attention?

If attentive listening signals care, haphazard listening expresses indifference. When we fail to listen, we are in effect telling the other that she is of no importance to us, that we have no time for her, that she doesn't count. Hospitious listening validates others; impatient or distracted listening discounts them.

Making Room, Creating Space

Author Margaret Guenther observes, "At its simplest, hospitality is a gift of space, both physical and spiritual, and like the gift of attentive listening, it is not to be taken lightly" (1992, p. 14). To offer hospitality is to offer sanctuary. Rooted in the notion of holiness, sanctuary is a safe place, or a place of holy refuge. Adoptions in which participants become a safe haven for each other are a cut well above the ordinary. It is remarkable to find safety in the fold of persons who hold the capacity to level dreams, and those who manage this coup are transformed by the trust they share. The safety we find in each other is especially meaningful because so many people outside the experience seem not to "get" what is going on. In the sanctuary of a hospitable relationship, we are protected from hazard and nurtured. Neither crowded nor rushed, we have a chance to catch our breath, spread out our stuff, and ponder our circumstances. No one is keeping score or cheapening the moment with expectations of payment. Hospitality of this quality sometimes feels almost miraculous.

Commenting on a surgical operation he observed, writer Brian Doyle offers insight that applies to the art of hospitality. "A great part of a surgeon's skill was the ability to create an operation as [she] went along, to change direction based on the changing nature of the problem being revealed, to be loosely astute rather than rigidly prepared" (2003, p. xxi). Surely making room for others involves preparation—readiness, we called it moments ago—but true readiness is a matter of remaining "loosely astute." Loosely astute people of goodwill are able to improvise and meaningfully respond to others based on what they have noticed and heard. Able to adapt on the fly, conveyors of hospitality are not easily defeated by setbacks. When one avenue is blocked, they alter their course and find another way. Their flexibility enables them to carve out room for others.

Hospitality happens best when offered with humility. We need humility because there is something in the needful other that tempts us to offer advice and direction. Overestimating our understanding of the other and her circumstance, we start cooking up ways to fix the challenges she faces and we end up crowding her. Numbers of well-meaning adoptive parents have unwittingly intruded on the emotional space of birthparents. Apartments in better neighborhoods have been rented, colleges promoted, and jobs offered. Most of these gestures have fallen flat in short order. They were intended as help, but they felt intrusive. Simple availability and attentiveness almost always accomplishes more than crusades of advice and direction.

So that is our brisk tour of hospitality. Succinctly stated, when goodwill, respect, and courage come alive through noticing, listening, and making room, an ethic of engagement is launched and possibilities for life-giving cooperation are opened. Full of promise and potential, hospitality changes things. As Professor Oden puts it, "When hospitality is extended or received, strange and amazing things can happen" (2001, p. 119).

CHAPTER 3

SAVORING HOSPITALITY'S WELCOME:
Through the Eyes of the Stranger

Something in me insists on approaching the subject of hospitality from the perspective of the host. When talk turns to hospitality, I immediately begin to mull over the challenges associated with making myself available to others. My mind does not happily entertain the idea that frequently *I am the other*. After all, as you will recall from the Introduction, I am either, rarely, the Good Samaritan or regularly, the religious stiff crossing the street. But the guy in need? Me? I don't think so. In the journey of adoption, I struggle to remember that I am as often a stranger as I am a host to strangers.

The "stranger" in adoption is the person who is out of his element, who is not in control, who is not at home in the circumstance. To varying degrees, he stands before his advantaged counterparts *unfamiliar*, *disconnected*, and *disentitled*. Not only is he largely unknown, he provides few clues about himself because he is out of context. He is short on what psychologist Randolph Severson calls "situatedness" (1998, p. 23). And no matter what he does to bolster his status, he cannot unilaterally rise above his dependence; his prospects are in the hands of those who are, at least for the moment, more powerful. Lacking familiarity, social context, and a sense of worthiness, adoption's stranger pitches camp along the institution's boundaries. He is on the outside looking in.

The notion that I am born to host diminishes my capacity to connect to others. To counter my over-identification with the benevolent, long-suffering host, I will report as the stranger in this chapter. In this voice, I speak for all of us—birthparents, adoptive parents, adoptive persons, and service providers alike—because, as we will explore in more detail in the next chapter, each of us will log some uneasy time as "the other" as our shared story winds its way through the decades. We will all know moments of unfamiliarity, disconnection, and disentitlement.

One thing is immediately clear as I take on this voice: When I am the stranger, I would rather not hear a lot of talk about how frightening or exotic strangers are. Sure, we all hear stories about weird and desperate strangers, but please, when I stand at your door, let's not get carried away with this "down and out" and "wild-eyed" business. That guy out there shuffling around on your porch? Consider the possibility he might be an angel in extraordinary disguise.

Unfamiliar

Don't kid yourself. I noticed your hesitation when we first met. You were wondering, "Who is this guy?" Sure, you most likely had a little information about me, a scouting report, so to speak—I know I had some about you—but until we met, you did not really know me. As far as you were concerned, all things were possible. Ax murderer? Saint? Collector of used books? Maybe I'd be on the ball, but you couldn't rule out the possibility that I was some kind of con artist.

I could tell you were suspicious. Your eyes gave you away. You were worried that I would be demanding and unreasonable. I understood your fear because, truth be known, I had the same worries as I sized you up, while you were sizing me up.

Of all the concerns attached to strangers, the lack of familiarity is the easiest to relieve. The remedy, obviously, is familiarity, and that happens when people spend time with each other. We learn more about a person's character from rubbing shoulders with them than we can ever learn on paper, and we assign greater credibility to that which we have seen firsthand. Everyone benefits when the principals have a chance to get to know each other. Prospective birthparents need to look into the eyes of would-be adoptive parents in order to know in their bones that these are effective people. Likewise, prospective adoptive parents need firsthand information early on so they can determine whether or not they wish to become involved and make a commitment to long-term interaction. With so much on the line, information is at a premium, and we are tempted to bear down and grill each other. Hospitality suggests that we not conduct an interrogation; we simply need to talk. Trust is most apt to grow when information tumbles out in natural, back-and-forth exchange; the manner in which information is exchanged may convey more than the information that is shared.

Disconnected

Already you were wary because I was unknown to you, and now it's clear that the look of distress on my face has added to your concern. Believe me, I wish I could wipe that look away, but I can't. I look uneasy because I am. Tell me, do you know how this thing is supposed to work? I hope so, because I don't! Out of place and short on allies, I feel out of my element. I showed up at someone else's party, and I am hugely self-conscious. Since I don't really know anybody, my instinct is to carve out a place by doing something useful. I'd like to earn my way into this thing, but what's useful in this situation? It's as if all the jobs were handed out before I arrived. What should I do? Maybe the best thing is to make myself scarce.

How do we gain a sense of connection? Shared experience builds connection, but how do we position ourselves to gain that experience? The generic role of guest offers a few clues. Everyday experience teaches that a prudent guest does not take advantage of his host's hospitality by lodging unreasonable requests. Rather, he expresses his needs clearly, pitches in on chores, voices hearty appreciation, and is careful not to overstay his welcome. Those insights help a little, but a richer approach to building connections is to think in terms of relatedness.

Fitting in is often more a function of who we are than what we do. Personality, that unique conglomeration of character, energy, priorities, and outlook, is often more important than behavior. The essential questions are "Who are we to each other?" and "Is there a 'we'?" If positive answers to these questions emerge as we spend time together, we begin to connect.

Disentitled

The worst thing about being a stranger—even worse than not knowing how to fit in—is the fact that I am totally dependent on your goodwill. You hold all the cards. That makes me nervous, really nervous. In fact, nervous doesn't touch it—being so dependent in a situation this important makes me a little crazy. I am trying so hard to be agreeable and inoffensive that I hardly recognize myself. Do you think me a buffoon? What makes this so difficult is that I can't presume a thing. I can offer suggestions, but I am not the one in charge. If I misread a situation and offend you, you might write me off forever. In this ridiculously eager-to-please mode, I feel demeaned. Admittedly, this state of mind is largely of my own making—I'm irrationally distressed by high-magnitude dependency—but knowing that brings no comfort. Truly, this is not easy for any of us. I know it's not easy to be the host, but honestly, I would trade those worries for my current anxieties in a heartbeat!

Because I lack standing, I worry about your opinion of me. I know how these things work: If you see me as important, I will be high on your list of priorities. On the other hand, if I am of only passing interest, soon I will have trouble catching your attention. It seems that "tangential" people almost always make their approach when there is something more pressing to attend to. I hope, then, that you will find me interesting and important. That is to say, I hope you will not find me incidental to all this, and, hence, inconvenient. I hope you will bear in mind how sensitive about this I am. As much as I long for connection, I do not want to be a burden to anyone. I am dialed into anything you might say or do that hints that you are putting up with me. I hope you will not see involvement with me as a duty to be carried out. I hope you are glad that I exist.

Most participants understand their interdependence with the others involved in an adoption and are quick to acknowledge their inherent importance. This recognition of the obvious bolsters everyone's standing. Sadly, a few begrudge this interdependence and refuse their counterparts any connection. Minimizing the significance of the others, some people leave them as they were—unfamiliar, disconnected, and disentitled.

Hospitality: Great News for Strangers

There is not much to like about being a stranger. Granted, there is an element of "fresh start" about it since one's past is largely unknown, but mostly it is a lonely and confusing state. It is demoralizing to be viewed with suspicion, and it is frustrating to be so dependent. Apart from finding the interior grace to cope with dependence, there is little one can do on one's own to find relief.

I know exactly what I need in order to feel better about all this—I need your sincere welcome. That would be great news for many reasons. For one thing, it would bring a spirit of grace and acceptance to our awkward beginnings. I don't know what I would do if your reception was cool and standoffish, but I don't particularly like my options. I could match stuffy with stuffy, I could set aside my dignity and slip into "suck up" mode, or I could kick the door down and demand a place at the table. None of these responses would get us off to a very good start. The relaxed ambiance of your hospitality, though, calms my edginess. By taking interest and signaling that you would like to get to know me, you restore a measure of my dignity.

Furthermore, your welcome helps me feel more grounded. It takes me a long way toward feeling that I have a place in this story, and that I have something to offer. Since you think of us as related because of our mutual commitment to a loved one, I no longer feel like an outsider or intruder.

Thankfully, your recognition of our relatedness gives me a measure of standing. That bit of generosity means that I am a valued participant, and that I actually belong in this situation. What a relief! That nascent sense of belonging allows me to let down my guard a little.

A welcoming response makes an enormous difference. As theologians Miroslov Volf and Dorothy Bass poetically put it, "Hospitality ushers the stranger across the threshold between the inside and outside" (2002, p. 137). That simple image captures much of the magic of hospitality. Having crossed the threshold, the stranger is suddenly more like a welcomed bride than a trespasser at the door.

How good it feels to be welcomed and included! Although our circumstance will always contain some uncertainties, I am beginning to feel a little more at home in this unnerving situation. I know that to be true because I am starting to think less about "you" and "me" and more about "us." I like that. It's even okay that I am not in control. I don't have to be in control as long as I know I will be taken into account. I am in the loop, I am a player, and I matter. Because of your gracious welcome, I dare to exhale in the dignity-restoring hope that I have a future in this relationship.

I will not soon forget your welcome. Forgive my sappiness, but your hospitality changes everything for me. All that initially struck me as bewildering, even as threatening, now seems manageable. Instead of feeling unimportant and suspect, I feel respected. The anguish of having no standing has been replaced with the genial prospect of belonging. No, I will not forget. I will do my best to rise to your generosity of spirit.

My time as "the other" is unnerving but valuable. It softens me. This tenderizing may in turn help me to become a more effective host, although that transfer of insight is not automatic. Whether or not it leads to improved hosting, my journey as the stranger expands both my self-awareness and my awareness of others. As Sarah York writes in *The Holy Intimacy of Strangers*, "The notion of intimacy with strangers poses an intriguing paradox: we encounter the familiar in the unfamiliar, the known in the unknown, the self in the other, and the other in the self" (2002, p. 4).

We are strangers together, you and I, both separated and oddly joined by our lack of familiarity. We have a lot to learn from each other. Thank you for noticing, listening, and making room for me. Maybe this will turn out okay.

CHAPTER 4

THE DYNAMIC POTENTIAL OF HOSPITALITY:
The Adoptive Child as Emerging Host

Healthy adoptions are alive with change. They teem with growth and shifts and transitions. They leapfrog, rest up, backtrack, and spin off in novel directions. Dynamic adoptions react, celebrate, repent, invent, and evolve. In the effort to "get it right," there is continuous tinkering and fine-tuning. Adoptions take root and deepen. To accommodate the emergence of the maturing child, these green-with-life families cannot help but sprout, swell, season, ripen, and yield. Though it may seem there are dormant seasons, healthy adoptions surge with life. They do everything but stay put.

How do we get at all this liveliness? How do we begin to think about the dynamism of adoptive families? One way to get our minds around the energy of adoptive family life is to catch its hospitious rhythms, the gestures of hosting and guesting that sashay through the years. Like the adoptive experience it enriches, hospitality presumes movement and change. Relational in its focus, it is well suited to explore the vitality of adoptive families.

The interplay of guesting and hosting is crucial to this consideration. Since the roles are passed back and forth and are sometimes exchanged discretely, it is often difficult to distinguish the guest from the host. The usual key is to discern who holds the advantaged position. Who is most at home in a particular phase or a given circumstance? Who is most sure-footed? In some instances, when everyone feels insecure, the ragged question becomes "Who among us is least uncomfortable?" Most of the time the host holds the strongest hand, and her advantage takes many forms. Sometimes it is raw authority, but it can also be a matter of practical resources, interpersonal connections, social status, personal presence, and social skill. Guests are never without power—the hospitable endeavor will fall flat without their cooperation—but they usually hold less of it than their counterparts. Adoptive participants are usually sensitive to the differential power they hold, especially when they are in the dependent position. If hosts mishandle this dynamic, things can quickly grow testy. Gifted hosts, on the other hand, manage their responsibilities so adroitly that their advantages are inconspicuous. Some are so skillful that they create the impression that the power dynamic has been inverted. Their grace is a gift to everyone involved.

The adoption journey never grows entirely familiar. Circumstances change and necessitate adjustments. Participants change, too, particularly the youngster. As she matures, new rounds of hospitality are required so this "new person" can be re-welcomed. Shifts in the guest-host dynamic surface as the child, originally the honored guest, matures into the one who does the welcoming. Her march toward hosting is often sporadic. One day she may be hesitant, the next eager. Some moves may be impulsive and bold while others are calculated and subtle. Occasionally she may revert to the cushy role of guest. Also, because the modern adoptive family system involves many participants, individuals may hold the host and guest role at the same time. A birthfather, for example, may simultaneously function as a guest of the adoptive parents and as host to the child.

We should note, too, that in adoptive clans where familiarity and trust is high, the dynamics of hospitality fade into the background. These families simply enjoy their relationships and interact naturally and un-self-consciously. Strangers no more, they are friends, and friendship does not reckon in terms of guest and host. An adoptive mother laughs, "Our sons' birthmoms really fit in around here. Each has a toothbrush and some toiletries in the drawer because it's easier to leave that stuff here than it is to carry it back and forth all the time." These high-trust families are puzzled when asked who initiates contact most commonly. After a moment of thought, they answer "All of us. We talk with each other often, and in the course of ordinary conversation, ideas bubble up."

Prenatal Hospitality

There is no doubt where adoptive hospitality begins: The first host is the mother who decides to sustain her pregnancy despite the fact that circumstances may be far from ideal. Another choice could be made, but as inopportune as things may be, she makes room for this unexpected one. It is a brave and consequential bit of hospitality that reverberates through many lives for many years.

In the best of circumstances, the hosting she offers is comprehensive. Recognizing that she will play the host role all too briefly, she savors the opportunity by securing prenatal health care and maintaining a healthy lifestyle. Other times the hosting may be more austere. Being the recipient of little if any hospitality herself, the pregnant woman may be hard pressed to muster much of it for the inconvenient stranger. Her disinclination toward hospitality is at least partially understandable. In the grimmest of situations, one is reminded of the phonetic connection between *host* and *hostility*. When it takes just about everything one has to stay afloat, a cheerful attitude about the assumption of responsibility for another cannot be presumed.

The baby, of course, is innocent of any difficulties associated with the pregnancy, so there is reason to hope, no matter how devastating circumstances may be, that the expectant mother can find it in her heart to respect the newcomer and offer a healthy sanctuary. Contrary to some preadoptive coaching, the prenatal task is not detachment. Rather, the spirit of hospitality encourages acknowledgment and connection. The hospitable premise is that the baby, as is true of guests in every situation, takes it all in. Guests are always sensitive to the extent of their welcome. The hospitious course is to enjoy her in all the affectionately goofy ways that parents ordinarily do. Hospitality-conscious adoption practitioners encourage pregnant parents to talk to their baby, pray for her, sing to her, and keep her posted on the progress of the local sports teams. Love this baby! Rub the tummy and affirm her. Offer her a favorite song to dance to. Give her a nickname. Take the burgeoning month-by-month profile pictures. Keep a journal. Prepare keepsakes and gifts. In short, the hospitious mandate is to fully attend to this tender guest and help her feel uterously welcome.

In many situations potential birthparents are also prenatal hosts to prospective adoptive parents. This role takes many of them by surprise because in so many of their other relationships they feel anything but powerful. In relation to prospective adoptive parents, however, the expectant mother is conspicuously powerful. Her hosting of the expected baby positions her as host to prospective adoptive parents, but her piggybacked status raises an important question: Is she appreciated in her own right, or is she instrumentally valued as the host to the expected child? The answer reveals much about the strength of their connection. If their interest in each other is a matter of utility, there is reason to wonder how things will hold up later on when their usefulness to each other slips into the background.

Preparing for the possibility of adoption is a daunting task for expectant parents, but the opportunity to choose the adoptive family is an interesting and exciting juncture in the process. It is a chance to situate the baby in an especially loving circumstance, though it is also a fearful project because candidates to adopt may misrepresent themselves and their intentions. Stakes could hardly be higher. There are many variables for expectant parents to consider as they appraise possible adoptive families. If they are serious about remaining involved, they do well to look for a family with a robust history of hospitality.

Once the family has been selected, the process of getting to know them begins. It is up to the potential birthparents to determine how much if any prenatal interaction there will be. As always, hosting carries risks and rewards. The desire to set a genial stage for what may turn out to be an enduring relationship has to be weighed against the hazard of shouldering the dreams of the hope-filled prospective adoptive parents. Bluntly stated, the singular task of the expectant parents is to determine the best outcome for their child, nothing more. Learning more about the family-in-waiting advances that goal, yet they must be careful that their concern for these appealing, needy persons does not color their thinking about what is best for their baby.

Some expectant parents find great relief and satisfaction in building an early connection to the prospective adoptive parents. Many are able to relax and enjoy the remainder of the pregnancy once they know a capable, loving family is on hand and is fully prepared to step into the parental role if needed. Prospective adoptive parents, after all, are enthusiastic and appreciative guests. For them, the incomparable days of expectancy are deliciously suspenseful, joyous, comical, and dramatic. Their excitement can energize a pregnancy that might otherwise feel uncelebrated.

Others, worried about setting into motion a set of activities that can be hard to reverse, keep their distance from the prospective adoptive parents. They recognize how easily the *possibility* of adoption can harden into an *expectation*. If this degeneration occurs, the contentment of connection is undermined by the feeling that there are strings attached. Conscientious facilitators work hard to prevent "expectation creep" by preserving the first family's options as long as possible. Effective planning always anticipates that parents may not move forward with adoption. This is true even with expectant parents who are "absolutely certain" about adoption because experience shows that they, too, may discover things are quite different once the baby is born.

The prenatal connection of prospective birth- and adoptive parents can be deleterious or advantageous. The difference depends on hospitality. If the interaction between the families is ulterior and somehow crowds, burdens, or obligates the first parents, the linkage is worrisome. On the other hand, if the interaction between the families is guided by genuine hospitality—if the attitudes of good-will, respect, and courage, and the behaviors of noticing, listening, and making room govern the circumstance—their interface will be satisfying. On those terms, the time they spend together will be mutually rewarding, and the prospective birthparents will retain all of their options.

Natal Hospitality

There is no arrival as dramatic as birth. Breathtaking and miracu-lous, it calls for lavish rounds of hospitality. The first expression of natal hospitality is the welcome the new parents extend to the child. This is not some ritual to efficiently get through so the important work of transition can be launched. Rather, the ideal is for the baby to luxuriate in an intimate, protracted milieu of appreciation.

We have a sad history in adoption of minimizing the importance of this first welcome. Instead of enjoying a hearty round of intro-ductions, our energy goes into moving the newcomer from one set of parents to the next as swiftly as possible. Typically we justify this elevation of adult interests over the baby's by downplaying her awareness of her surroundings.

The arrival of new life is always momentous, and the prospect of adoption significantly adds to the emotional weight of the circum-stance. In addition to wholeheartedly welcoming the newborn, the spirit of hospitality suggests the new parents and the prospective adoptive parents need to work out their interactions and figure out how available they will be to each other. They may have forged meticulous plans for this time together, yet the reality of it often morphs into an almost wordless dance with partners improvising their moves as they read each other's cues. This interplay is mar-velous to observe when they are in sync, and excruciating when they are not. Natal hospitality is so important that we will return to it in Chapter 6.

Postnatal Hospitality (Impermanent Care)

Once the baby has been entrusted to the temporary care of the prospective adoptive family, a new and anxious phase is entered. Legalities vary, but in many jurisdictions birthparents in effect sublet their hosting role to the chosen family. While the around-the-clock responsibility of looking after the baby is transferred to the would-be adoptive parents, bottom line authority is retained by the first parents.

From the perspective of hospitality, this is a crucial and complicated phase; a time of high pressure that sets a tone for all that follows. A momentous shift is apparently in the works, and everyone has lots of sorting out to do. Against a backdrop of mental and physical exhaustion, emotions need managing and new routines need to be ironed out. Three questions stand out. What can be done to help the baby get used to her new surroundings? How will the birthfamily tolerate separation from the baby? And how will the prospective adoptive parents handle their hosting responsibilities in the face of uncertainty and anxiety?

This season of uncertainty tests the character of everyone involved. The various factors that necessitate hospitality and make it so helpful—fatigue, grief, uncertainty, and novelty—are also factors that wear people down and make it difficult to offer. With the ultimate decision hanging in the balance, some prospective adoptive parents report that they "don't dare to exhale." The reflex is to hold things in rather than relax and let go. How does one go about hosting a cherubic stranger who presents so much emotional danger? Further, the inherently confusing nature of the circumstance must be sorted out. How does one whose hosting authority is borrowed play host to those who lent it?

Adoptive mother Jenny Robertson reports that they were never tempted to play it safe and hold their freshly welcomed daughter, Kaia, at an emotional distance during this risky phase. For this naturally hospitable mother, that was a prospect "more horrible than getting burned." She explains, "Kaia was in such good condition when Christine put her in our care. She was so proud of her baby girl, and of herself and the job she had done, and her love was amazing to witness. She spent two days in the hospital loving and caring for Kaia, and making sure that Kaia got to know us, too. Kaia moved through the transition so well, mainly, I think, because Christine embraced her so totally when she was born, and because she had the strength to include us too so we wouldn't be strangers to her daughter. Her wisdom and her complete and total love for Kaia put us in awe. She's an amazing mom."

For Jenny, the best way to deal with the anxiety was to stay in close contact and speak with candor. When, in the course of trimming Kaia's nails, Jenny nicked the baby's finger and drew blood, she promptly confessed to Christine, "I'm not the mother you thought I was!" But Christine was reassuring in her response. If anything, the confession deepened her endorsement of these carefully selected adoptive parents, for implicit in the confession were messages of devotion to Kaia, respect for Christine as a birthparent, and an impulse to keep her informed.

For those with eyes to see it, some babies enter their new family signaling that they are missing their first family. Nicole Miller, an exceptionally observant mother with a master's degree in biology, noticed that her son Scott was uncomfortable when he first joined them. Even though the goodwill between the families could not be greater and the transition of care had been virtually free of stress, the baby was not comfortable. "Things were interesting to him, but they were not what he expected. He'd look at the stuff around him longer than you would expect. He seemed surprised by things, a little alarmed, a little scared, even." She and her husband responded with extra cuddling time and rocking him more often than they might have otherwise. "I told Scott that I understood his confusion—it made complete sense to me given the changes he'd encountered—and I wasn't taking it personally. We all prefer the familiar to the unfamiliar." When Scott's birthmother, Katie, visited them two weeks later and held him, he visibly let down his guard and relaxed. "That brought me peace of mind. I knew then that I wasn't crazy, that I wasn't imagining all of this." Nicole continued hospitably, "When human beings are valued by others, their value rises in everyone's eyes and they feel better. Patients in hospitals who have lots of visitors are treated better than patients with few." This remarkable student of adoption concludes, "I'm his mother. There's no doubt about that because even as an infant he reserves his worst for me— he knows in his bones that nothing could interfere with my love for him. Since we are so connected, I am able to watch with interest as he interacts with various people. At 10 months he is wary of people he doesn't know very well, yet he reaches out to Katie instantly even when he hasn't seen her for several weeks. We're pleased that his first family remains in his life to comfort him and appreciate him. His life will be better because there are so many people who love him. So will ours."

Like all new parents, mothers and fathers in these exotic, unsettled circumstances face a hospitality dilemma. They naturally want to expand the welcome to include the many people who are excited about the arrival of the baby, yet they also want to settle into predictable patterns for her sake. Their challenge is to balance the pleasing excitement of well-wishers against the baby's need for consistency.

At the same time the hope-filled prospective adoptive parents are doing everything in their power to help the baby feel at home and are working hard to manage their anxieties about parenting—not to mention those attached to the ultimate outcome—they are also attending to the empty-armed birthfamily. It is a time that calls for excellent communication, but this, too, asks a great deal of them. Sometimes the on-duty parents are too worn out to minister to their compatriots; it is the last thing they feel like doing. The sadness of the grieving birthfamily stirs feelings of guilt and saps their dwindling energy, and they are tempted to dodge them. There are other times when respect for the other's privacy impedes communication. It is as if these tired parents need a sixth sense to know when to offer reassurance and when to step back and provide emotional space.

Another remarkably hospitable adoptive mother, Donna Eberle, recalls the difficulty of this phase. "When it was all up in the air,

Kaitlin's birthmother, Holly, turned to me for comfort. It was a very difficult situation to be in. My joy, after all, was her pain. No one knows what to do in a situation like that. Our reflex was to be inclusive. We included Holly in everything we did. We became part of her family, and she became part of ours. We found our way through together."

Looming over the temporary phase of care is the possibility that the prospective birthparents may call for their daughter or son's return. Because that prospect casts such a large shadow over the adoptive experience, we will take a closer look at the importance of hospitality in that circumstance in Chapter 7.

The Hospitality of Childhood (Birth to 8 Years)

Once the torch of legal responsibility is passed to the adoptive parents, they become the master hosts. More than any other factor, their effectiveness in this role will govern the long-term joy and satisfaction of the arrangement; the greatness of an adoption cannot exceed the degree of hospitality offered by the adoptive parents. It is up to them to energize the overall arrangement by demonstrating hospitious attitudes and behavior, and the heartiness of their welcome will echo through all of the other relationships woven into the adoption.

As master hosts, they take the lead in setting precedent and establishing the norms in their relationships with the various players involved. Of particular importance is the welcome they extend to their child's immediate birthfamily, for that relationship cradles all of the other interactive possibilities. If that core relationship brims with hospitality, plenty of room will be provided for other connections to flourish as well.

There is more to the adoptive parents' hospitality than the privilege of welcoming others into their family sphere. They are hosts, but they are also advocates for the honored guest. That responsibility means the ball is always in their court; it is up to them to stir things up if communication lags. They are instigators who serve their children by promoting regular contact with loved ones. When adoptive parents bless the connection between their child and her birthfamily and deem it healthy and desirable, they create an atmosphere in which it is safe for the child to express her interests and act on them. Adoptive parents also play an important role by facilitating their child's communication and contact with the birthfamily, an especially helpful boost when it compensates for limitations related to age, personality, or lack of courage. One wise adoptive mother reports that she calls the birthfamily to smooth the way prior to dropping her son off for a visit. "It's a little tricky because I don't want to imply that they are in some way not up to handling things, yet I want to do all I can to set them up for success. I might hint, 'This kid needs to eat regularly.' If I'm feeling blunt, I might warn 'Woe to anyone who goes 15 minutes past an expected food stop with this young man!'"

Familiarity between the parents and the child naturally grows from year to year. Fully realized hospitality creates the ideal space where a youngster feels completely at home—utterly claimed, unconstrained by tentacles of parental possessiveness, and rightfully presumptive of a place at the table. Welcomed, accepted, and treasured, she has a sound base from which she can explore the world around her. Moving forward, adoptive hospitality means noticing, listening to, and validating the youngster's emerging voice.

The most important feature of the hospitable approach to adoption is that it makes room for adoptive children to move beyond the passivity that has long characterized their circumstance. It invites them to shed the role of indebted guest and grow into the role of ultimate host. As we clear the way for this growth, we welcome these developing youngsters as coauthors of the family story. Commensurate with their developing capabilities, they join other family members, birth and adoptive, in defining, shaping, and energizing key relationships. No longer is adoption something that happened to them some while back. Instead, the children of hospitious adoption actively participate in shaping their life course.

This shift in how we think and talk about adoption holds the potential to radically alter the way it is experienced. Our conceptualizations inform our expectations. When the idea that adoptive children are not just "along for the ride" sinks in, that in fact they are better understood as emerging hosts and not as people forever subject to the actions of others, we open many new possibilities for them. Consider, for example, a daughter's curiosity about her birthfamily. From the emerging host perspective, it makes no sense to view this interest as disloyal to her parents. Rather, that interest signals that she is growing into her role as host and is appropriately working to understand and integrate the various factors that contribute to her personhood. In this way hospitality brings new vitality to our aspiration that adoption be child-centered. By enabling us to keep the end in mind from the beginning, hospitality creatively alters the day-to-day experience of adoption.

Adoptive children are only going to have room to maneuver if their parents make that room, and that is most likely to happen when parents feel secure in their roles. Donna Eberle, the adoptive mother who commented earlier in favor of inclusion, has that security. She reports, "People often ask us how we dare to have so much contact with our daughter's birthfamily. What people don't understand is how connected we are to our daughter. Our relationship to that kid is so amazing that there is absolutely no room for insecurity." Adoption expert Severson speaks to the importance of this security as only he can.

> Adoptive parents need not fear the birthparents, for the love that a child will feel for these mysterious strangers, whose presence in reality, no matter how erratic or infrequent it might be, confirms that roots are real while reassuring of unbroken continuity with the rest of the human race, in no way diminishes the love that the child will feel for the parents whose strength and love surrounds them in the way of a blanket on a cold winter night. Their parents' arms give them security; their parents' eyes give them hope. Their parents' dreams give them a future. And in the case of an open adoption, their parents' courage gives them a past and thus an opportunity to heal their hearts.

Love, not the law, is what makes an adoptive parent real."
(1994, p. 266)

That is the sort of security that enables the aforementioned Robertsons, Jenny and her husband Ian, to put a picture on their refrigerator of daughter Kaia and her birthmother, Christine, locked in a loving gaze. It is a quiet yet formidable statement to all who enter their home: "Our baby has never known a moment when she was not fully loved, and we couldn't be more pleased."

We often underestimate the awareness young children have about adoption. An especially attentive adoptive mother, Katrina Tripp, tells of some remarkable moments when her daughter Kaylie was 4. They were tending to some flowers and Katrina was bent over reaching for a weed when Kaylie confessed, "Mom, I think I love my birthmom." When Katrina looked up to respond to the comment, she immediately discerned that Kaylie was studying her with extraordinary attention, on the lookout for verbal and nonverbal information. She assured Kaylie that her love was a great thing, that she hoped she would love all of the important people in her life. Kaylie's face lit up at that response. Unencumbered, she literally went skipping down the garden path, a very relieved young lady. Reflecting on that exchange, Katrina declares, "It was clearly a test. Adoption was very much on her mind, and she had to know whether or not this was something that could be talked about. That moment changed everything. It lightened the air, and we've been talking about adoption freely ever since."

Later that year the two of them were resting in a hammock together, affectionately chatting about assorted subjects when Kaylie began sobbing. According to Katrina, it was not an ordinary sort of crying; it was "heart wrenching." Once she regained her composure, Kaylie explained, "I don't know why I'm crying. I'm just sad. I feel like something is missing. I love you and Dad—you're my parents—but I wish it wasn't this way." Her tears challenge conventional thought. If we think that young children are oblivious to the fullness of adoption with its lush texture of sadness and joy, we do well to reconsider.

By Katrina's account, Kaylie's emergence as host began when she was 7. "I knew we were moving into a new phase when she came walking into the room one day carrying my address book and declared, 'I'm going to call Nancy.'" With her mother's assistance, the call was made, and precedent was set. Kaylie is a little unusual in her desire to make the call herself. Commenting on phone contact in childhood, many other adoptive parents report that the typical process is for the youngster to declare, "Mom, we need to call Cindy." Decoded, the statement means, "I want you to call Cindy and get some conversation going. Then, when things are going well, I want you to give me the phone and I'll take it from there." Adoptive children want to know that their first family is okay. They also enjoy keeping their birthparents posted on their accomplishments, and it is not beyond them to invite that extended family to come and watch as they exhibit their competence at a concert or ballgame.

One more Kaylie story: In the course of a visit with her birthmother, Nancy, discussion turned to a bit of discipline that had recently been directed toward Kaylie. As the story wound down, Kaylie tilted her head toward her birthmother and asked, "What would you have done?" Surprised but quick on her feet, Nancy responded, "Whoa, don't even go there! I'm lined up with your Mom and Dad!" Many adoptive families report that Nancy's response is one of the benefits of continuing connection. They appreciate having their decisions backed up by, as the Tripps put it, "a much cooler, more contemporary" person holding high standing in the eyes of the youngster.

While it is safe to posit that highly hospitable adoptions enjoy more interaction than less congenial arrangements, it is difficult to speak of typical interactive patterns because they are so affected by the personalities involved. One family, for example, reports traveling to another state to visit their shy adolescent son's birthmother. It was a visit that he had looked forward to for a long time, but true to his nature, he rushed to the conversational sidelines once the opportunity arrived, unable to express his thoughts and feelings. His confident younger sister fills every social vacuum, and she wasted no time pouncing on the opening. To most of those gathered that morning, she saved the day and turned an awkward circumstance into a rollicking encounter. In the eyes of this young man, however, his brassy little sister had stolen his show.

We encourage all of the participants in adoption to take broad interest in the other family, especially when there are other children involved. Adoptive parents appreciate it when birthfamilies pay attention to all of the children in the family. Likewise, birthfamilies appreciate it when their other children are included and respected as equals. This inclusive approach has produced many serendipitous results. When it was time for Emily Joseph, for example, to enlist a sponsor for her confirmation at church, she asked her younger sister's birthmother, Kristy, to fill the role. The two of them have grown close, and recently Kristy took Emily to "Little Sibs Day" at her university.

On the other hand, adoptive mother of four Terri Bieszka has turned our advice on end. "Nobody's lacking for attention around here, that's for sure," she states. "We suggest to the birthfamilies that they go ahead and zero in on their son or daughter. It's great for them to acknowledge everybody in the family, but we also want them to recognize that there's a particular kid itching to spend some special time with them."

According to adoptive mother Carol Stadden, who more than once has stood at the airport with a lump in her throat as she watched a daughter or son board a plane to spend a week with a geographically distant birthparent, "You don't sweat the small stuff; *connection trumps comfort*." Better, in her view, to risk some transitory clash of values than to risk disconnection.

It is difficult for adoptive parents to determine how assertive they ought to be in their efforts to include the birthfamily. One of the unhappiest and least hospitable words in adoption is *intrusion*. If initiatives to get together are not reciprocated or if a bit of hesitation is detected, many are tempted to back off. In many ways this is a respectful reaction, though there are times when one wonders if their retreat has more to do with their wish for convenience than with serving the interests of their youngster. Their concern about intrusion poses a classic hospitality conundrum that pits important dimensions of hospitality against each other. The adoptive parents, after all, have hospitable obligations to their child and to their child's birthparents. That is a fruitful path as long as everyone is like-minded, but what are they to do when their interests diverge? On one hand, the spirit of hospitality instructs them to offer others plenty of room and to avoid crowding them. That principle suggests it might be better to leave disengaged birthparents alone. When it comes to providing hospitality to their children, though, adoptive parents have a responsibility to play the role of advocate and to do their best to secure ongoing access to the people who are important to the children. The "connection trumps comfort" maxim is helpful in resolving this tangle. If there is to be error, let it be in the direction of connection.

The Hospitality of Pre-Adolescence and Adolescence (8 to 18 Years)

With the relatively simple days of childhood behind them, many children grow braver about expressing their wishes. This is the phase when children in hospitious families take more initiative and assume greater responsibility for their adoptive relationships.

One might suppose that this Internet generation of adoptive adolescents would make great use of this ubiquitous resource to communicate with their birthfamilies. It turns out that for many of these young people the Internet is not the tool of choice. Another insight from Carol Stadden explains this surprising fact. "Our kids are certainly proficient on the Net, but they greatly prefer to hear their birthmother's voice."

There are times when birthparents happily fill the role of host. Kaitlin Eberle is situated in an especially dynamic adoption. Her parents and birthmother have established a close friendship, so she has ready access to the important people in her life. Her relationship with her birthmother, Holly, is meaningful and tender. She and her sister Lauren were in Holly's wedding, and Holly is frequently in the crowd when either of the girls has a concert or sporting event. As Kaitlin's 10th birthday approached, she held hopes that the occasion might be robustly commemorated. She aspired to a major party, and she wanted all of her closest friends to attend. In the course of routine conversation—they chat weekly—Holly suggested that the party be held at her house because she has a pool. Actually that was a bit of an understatement because they all knew it was not just any old pool; it was a pool featuring a panoramic view of Lake Michigan. That was easily the best idea generated, so the plan was put into motion. When the big day arrived, however, the weather was chilly and foreboding. But weather proved no match for family devotion. Recognizing that something needed to be done to offset nature's provocation, Holly's husband promptly rented a tent to put over the pool along with an outdoor heater to keep the guests warm. Needless to say, the entire birthday entourage felt very special, and the party was a memorable success.

Kaitlin's families are happily intertwined, and they interact with confidence and ease. Adoptive mother Donna notes that the locus of hospitality has shifted over time. "Now that Holly is fully settled into a domestic scene of her own—she has a loving husband and a 2-year-old son who is wild about Kaitlin and who is a great joy to us all—she plays the host more than we do. They have a beautiful home, enjoy having people visit them, and are great at making people feel at home. They're so good at it that lately we most often go there."

The Varley family thoroughly enjoys their relationships with the birthfamilies of their son and daughter. At the time of this writing, adoptive mother Barb and daughter Colleen were making plans to travel so they could help Colleen's birthmother look after a newborn that she had just welcomed into her family by adoption. Colleen is a delightfully social 16-year-old who places high value on all of her relationships and nurtures them. When Barb was asked, "What would happen if you had a different view of all this and somehow thwarted Colleen's interest in her birthfamily?" she gasped. "Oh," she said, taking a moment to recover from such an unthinkable question, "that wouldn't be good."

In hospitable families, inhospitable loose ends stand out. An adoptive mother tells of her 10-year-old son's frustration regarding his uninvolved birthfather. During preparations for bedtime, a time when conversation turns to matters of the heart in many households, this young man put his hands on his hips and demanded of his mother, "Don't put me off on this; I need an answer. Tell me, what kind of person would not want to know a kid like me? Where is my birthfather? Why is he not part of my life?" He is not alone. Children in incommunicative adoptions have no choice but to settle for little, but children who are blessed with lots of information are often not content until every card is on the table.

The Hospitality of Emancipation (Adulthood)

In the early years of open adoption, we believed we had solved the loyalty conflict that many adoptive persons found so painful in the closed system. We thought the issue was defused when we reworked the birthparent-adoptive parent dynamic from adversarial to cooperative. No doubt we brought some relief to the issue, but we surely did not eliminate it. The question "Who is my family?" sits at the doorstep of each adoptive person, patiently awaiting an answer. Is his primary alliance with his adoptive family or with his birthfamily? Or does he define family to encompass all of them? The "all of the above" solution appeals to many. There are times, though, when that answer is difficult to pull off. A holiday like Thanksgiving, for example, may call the question. Does one eat turkey and stuffing with the adoptive family or the birthfamily? At least one adoptive adult is determined to remain inclusive. Declares 25-year-old Jessica Hoyt, "As soon as I get a decent-sized place, they're all coming to my house for Thanksgiving, and that's how it's going to be!"

Jessica is happy to have two mothers to turn to, though her birthmother April reports with a chuckle, "Nowadays it isn't always to her advantage." With an identical chuckle, Jessica confirms the mischief of that observation. "Sometimes they gang up on me!" she explains. "In some ways they are quite different, but they're both mothers and they think the way mothers think." Her mothers are accustomed to working together. If they have concerns about Jessica's health or her dating circumstances, they are, in her words, "back and forth on the phone staying on top of things." Jessica learned through the years that if she shared information with one mother, she had most likely shared it with both. The three of them are a playful trio. If they are at a restaurant together, Jessica takes pleasure in telling the waitress, "This is my mother," and pausing for effect before adding, "and this is my other mother."

Adulthood is a time when some adoptive persons attend to unfinished business. One young man reports that he is ready now to make an effort to connect to his birthfather. Although he was raised in a hospitious circumstance, he knew very little about his birthfather, and it bothered him. As a teenager he had pursued the subject gingerly because his questions clearly bothered his birthmother and left her sad, but he feels less constrained as an adult. "It's hard to put into words," he muses, "but it's almost as if I have more authority now. I'm not going to ignore my birthmother's feelings about this, but I need to do what I need to do." He admits to feeling "a little anxious" about "rounding off" his adoption by searching for his birthfather, but he is pleased to have the support of his family as he moves forward.

For that young man and others like him, emancipation is a long-awaited moment. They are eager to take things fully into their hands and arrange their relationships exactly to their liking. For many others, though, at least early on, emancipation changes very little.

An adoptive mother reports that her role as instigator continues into her son's adulthood. The chemistry between her grown son and his birthmother could not be better, yet they continue to need a boost. "When they get together, it's magic. Each of them is so happy. They talk and talk and talk, and it is obvious that they are delighted to be together." Since they are in a hospitious circumstance and live close to each other, one would suppose they are in frequent contact. Not so, according to the adoptive mom. "Their personalities are very similar," she explains. "They are very gentle, lovable persons, and there is something in their nature that makes them very reluctant to impose themselves on others. They are so receptive to each other, but neither is inclined to initiate contact. The only time they get together is when I orchestrate a meeting."

The adoptive person's emergence greatly affects the people around him. Sandy Hinkle and Bonnie, the birthmother of one of her sons, have established an enduring friendship. They entered their relationship with little common ground—they were different from each other in many ways—but their shared bond to a remarkable son brought them together in a very deep way. Now they are doppelgangers, fused by mother's love for the same rambunctious young fellow. They understand each other in ways that no one else can. Their years together have been lively and rich, and they report that they are looking forward to the day when they can be "grandmas together."

An adoptive mother observes that an important dimension of her daughter's pushing away during adolescence involves strengthening her connection to her birthfamily. "This is a deep need for her. She has longed for greater connection for many years, but geographic distance has made it difficult. No doubt she'll move to get closer to them. To be honest, it's a bit scary for us, but we understand this is something she needs to do and we support her efforts along these lines. You never know how things will turn out, but we're confident that in the end she will see all of us as her family."

An adoptive father predicts movement in another direction. He confided that he expects there will be some changes when his children come of age. The most significant development he foresees concerns their son and daughter's siblings who remained in the care of their first parents. "I think we'll see a lot more of those kids. I've sensed for a long time that they wished they could be a bigger part of our family, and I think they'll use the freedom of adulthood to move closer to our family."

The dynamism of adoption will continue through the adult decades. The adult adoptive person, standing on her own at last, may settle into the satisfactions and rigors of hosting for long stretches, but these routines may well be affected by the successive milestones of family life—marriages, pregnancies, health crises, moves to new locations, and deaths. It remains to be seen, but hope is strong that the genial spirit of hospitality will course through the generations that follow.

Derailed Hospitality

Hospitality can slip the track in innumerable ways. Several years ago colleagues from another state called to vent their frustration about an inhospitable event they had endured. They reported that they had worked very hard to find a hospitious family for a baby with cognitive disabilities. It took time and effort, but in the end, to their great satisfaction, they found an outstanding, welcoming family, and the adoption went forward. They noted that although nature had shortchanged this youngster in some important ways, it had offered a measure of compensation by giving him a fabulous head of hair. By all accounts, it was truly out-of-the-ordinary hair, and the adoptive parents absolutely gloried in it. Can you imagine, asked the indignant professionals, their dismay when their son returned from his first visit with the birthfamily with a brush cut?

An adoptive family tells about the time when their daughter's birthmother unilaterally decided in the course of an overnight visit that it was time for the 7-year-old to meet her birthfather for the first time. When it came to her attention that he had a family reunion planned for the next day, she resolved to crash the party. As it turned out, someone tipped off the birthfather that his daughter would be there, and he reacted by fortifying himself with several rounds of alcohol. The encounter could not have gone worse, and the adoptive parents mourn the fact that an impulsive decision soured an important relationship for their daughter before it ever had a chance to get started.

Over the years birthparents from many regions have written and asked for suggestions because their adoptive relationships had collapsed. One birthmother explained that she had selected a family that thoroughly impressed her with their warmth and their eagerness to enter a long-term relationship with her. The fact that he was a minister in her denomination was frosting on the adoption cake because it gave her absolute confidence that they would be true to their word. She was alarmed, though, when after a year of contact they stopped taking her calls. Convinced that she had unwittingly offended them, she mailed a heartfelt letter apologizing for whatever she had done to upset them. When their response came in the form of a letter from their attorney threatening legal action if she made additional efforts to contact them, she was crushed.

Any breakdown of hospitality is sad, but the most forlorn are those that damage the hopes of children. One set of parents lost their connection to their 6-year-old daughter's birthfamily when they said no to a discomforting proposal. Her birthgrandparents hoped she might spend a week with them even though another member of their extended family—a young male just out of prison—had just moved in with them for lack of alternatives. Although the adoptive parents expressed their unwillingness to go along with the plan as tactfully as they could, the birthgrandparents took their refusal as an indication of distrust. Offended, they broke off contact. As they saw it, their involvement was an all-or-nothing proposition. If their judgment was subject to question, they were not interested in maintaining the relationship. When their granddaughter made subsequent calls imploring them to visit her, they made excuses and put her off.

It is impossible for families who adopt more than one child to have identical relationships with the birthfamilies of their children. That fact never sets well with the in-house fairness officers, the children. One family that was well-connected to one birthmother but largely disconnected from the other decided to solicit the involvement of the disengaged birthmother. They were moved to action because their 7-year-old son, John, was sad to miss out on the excitement his younger brother was enjoying. They wrote several letters gently explaining their hope that she would get in touch with them, but these inquiries went unanswered. Finally John took personal charge of the project and wrote a letter in his own poignant words. "Dear Birthmother Jane, How are you? I think about you a lot, but I don't know if you're ok. Are you ok? I am mostly ok, but I am sad sometimes because I miss you. Could you please please please call me or write to me? P.S.: Do you remember that my birthday is next month? I love you. John." That letter drew a terse note to the adoptive parents from his birthmother. "I am John's birthmother, and I know what is best for him. The best thing for him is to not have contact with me. Please leave me alone. Jane."

The hopes of children are damaged, too, when adoptive parents project their fears on them. When an adoptive father gruffly makes the case that his children have no interest in birthparents because "they never talk about them," the evidence is hardly convincing. The edgy tone of voice, in fact, supports another hypothesis: namely, that this is a household where it is not safe to talk about adoption.

These stories illustrate that hospitality cannot be presumed. There are times when participants treat each other with little or none of it, and the price is high. The toll exacted in these hospitality breakdowns is reckoned in degrees of disconnection, with total disengagement being the most costly outcome. When adoptions occur inhospitably and the parties are disengaged, children inhabit a world of shrunken prospects.

Clearly, hospitality sweetens the adoptive experience of children. It expands their sphere of loving relationships, and it empowers them. While it is pleasing to envision children as emerging hosts, we must recognize that it is not a simple thing for a child to move into a more active role. Some will prefer to leave decisions in the hands of others more accustomed to making them, and who can fault them? Making decisions and leading the way, after all, is hard work. What is more, it carries the hazard of stepping on the toes of important people. Other adoptive youngsters, bolder or in some instances more self-absorbed, may revel in the opportunity. They may declare their wishes with little awareness or concern for the sensitivities of the others involved. That prospect calls for an important clarification. The emerging host paradigm does not mean that adoptive children suddenly run the show. They are encouraged to express themselves, but their ideas need to be negotiated with their parents who retain authority and oversight. Parents winnow the proposals of their children and encourage or discourage plans according to their merit. In healthy families, the amount of maneuvering room parents grant is commensurate to the maturity of their children.

As the children in hospitable adoptions gradually work their way toward management of their relationships, we need to remember that it is not up to them to make it all work. Their participation is meant to be an opportunity, not a burden, and the adults remain responsible for sustaining the hospitable nature of each adoption. As the child's needs, interests, and activities change over time and wax and wane in intensity, it falls to the adults to make whatever adjustments may be necessary. Adults need to be consistent and dependable so the children can remain, in the rightful manner of children, delightfully spontaneous and mysteriously inconsistent.

CHAPTER 5

HOSPITALITY'S SWEETEST FRUIT:
Feeling at Home with Each

Susan knew in her heart of hearts that she was not ready to look after a baby, so she pushed all signs of pregnancy out of her consciousness. The idea of having a baby was, literally, unthinkable. So, when the stomach cramps that inspired a worried dash to the hospital turned out to be six pounds of new life, she had some serious soul-searching to do. No matter how she looked at it, she kept coming back to the idea of adoption, and now, resting in her maternity room, she was plowing through portfolios of prospective adoptive parents. About halfway into the third photo album she announced, "Here they are; this is the family. I don't have to look at more." A call was made, and Jack and Deb rushed to the hospital to meet this enlivened new mother. Spontaneously crying and laughing and divulging personal details, they hit it off immediately. Watching them interact, one would suppose they had known each other a long time.

Days later, as we explored in a more relaxed setting Susan's thoughts and feelings about her baby's future, her story took fuller shape. Her parents had divorced when she was young. That meant her mother had to work a couple of jobs to keep their little family afloat. Exhausted, Mom had little energy to fuss over Susan and her sister; the kids had to largely fend for themselves. Susan explained, "I did really well at school, but no one seemed interested. So I imagined that I had parents who were paying attention, and they were very pleased." After pausing to let that remarkable childhood strategy sink in, she added, "And you know what? When I was looking through the portfolios and encountered Jack and Deb? There they were; I've been thinking about them all my life."

Clearly, Susan felt at home with the couple she chose to raise her son. The effortless familiarity she enjoyed with them brought her great peace of mind. The quality of their connection did not diminish her sense of loss—that was piercing and acute—but it did significantly reduce her anxiety. Her heart was heavy, but importantly, she was not racked with worry.

Susan is not alone in finding succor in the sensation of at-homeness; authentic acknowledgment and acceptance is something we all long for. The particular wonder of hospitality is that it opens a path to this prospect. When hospitality works, people feel at home. Likewise, when adoption works, children feel at home. What adoption in its highest forms seeks and what hospitality at its best produces is the inimitable comfort of feeling of "at home."

It's easy to overlook the significance of hospitality. After all, there is not much flourish or flash about noticing, listening, and making room. Our view of at-homeness parallels how we see water; we pay little attention to it when either is readily available. The moment we sense it is in short supply, however, little else counts. Our words for its absence are telling: *homesick, estranged, homeless,* and—particularly potent in the context of adoption—*orphan.* The heart not at-home knows little peace and sets few roots.

We long to be at home, for in the best of circumstances home is a sanctuary. It offers refuge and holy protection. Home is the one place where we know, without doubt, that we belong. At home there is no need to pretend that we are better than we are; we have nothing to prove. Surrounded with our people—with "our kind" as we sometimes say—we are unconditionally accepted. We count, we matter, and we will be heard and attended to. It's not that everything we do meets with approval—we may, in fact, encounter the keenest criticism from those who know us best and care for us the most—but our essential self is safe and deeply accepted.

Not only is home a place where we are claimed for better or worse, it is also the setting where we are familiar with the scheme of things. Because our norms were shaped in these surroundings, it's the place where things are done the way we figure they ought to be done. We know how things work, and we fall easily into routines and rhythms. There is nothing to match the sweetness of being at home.

In Dutch we find the word *gezellig*, a word retained through immigrant generations because it conveys something important for which there is no satisfactory English equivalent. It is often interpreted as "cozy," though those who know the word realize that substantially more is implied. *Gezellig* suggests deep contentment, a palpable sense that all is well with those we love. One popular translation is "togetherness that knows no time."

Indeed, our sense of being at home is both time-full and timeless. Home is our source and our destination. As the sum of countless formative influences, home shapes our present and future. It is our foundation and our base for ongoing operations. In the best of circumstances, home is where we logged time as the center of the universe, where everything we did was cause to marvel. First smile, first step, first cannonball off the diving board, first graduation—all were celebrated at home. In those surroundings, it occurs to us that we might just be lovable. We learn what is trustworthy and true, and we learn the importance of commitments with their attendant privileges and obligations. Home is a vessel for transgenerational continuity, our participation in the ongoing processes of life.

For all its potential, many people find home a tricky matter. Geographic transience, momentous reconfigurations of central relationships, and the searing hurts inflicted all too commonly within the intimacies of family life all challenge our sense of it. Little wonder, then, that surprising numbers of people are ambivalent about returning home for the holidays.

For many adoptive people, there is extra work to be done before they are able to feel at home, for in even the warmest of circumstances their stories begin with disconnection. So remarkable a dislocation is existentially provocative and is not easily sloughed off.

Adoption is a formidable fact of life to contend with as they work to craft a sense of identity. For them, personal history is multi-layered, and so is the sensation of familiarity. Where does the story begin? Does memory begin with childhood, or do cellular memories somehow precede them? And what feels most familiar? Does it come down to years of shared experience—the road trip to Yellowstone, Grandma's ribald humor, and Sunday morning doughnuts—or is it the visceral, cut-from-the-same-cloth congruence of genetic kin? The contemplative adoptive person wonders, "Who are my people?"

As an emergent host, an adoptive young person's task is to ascertain his place in the world. Where does he fit in? In what contexts does he feel in sync? To whom does he belong? Where does he feel most at home? Toward this end he will need to clarify, reconcile, and integrate the comforts and complications of history and familiarity. There is no set path to resolution. Some give it little thought or effort while others find the challenge unnerving, relentless, and unyielding. The really fortunate ones find ways to merge all of the factors into a larger, harmonious whole.

Sara Vander Haagen, an early beneficiary of a hospitious approach to adoption, began working on this quest for coherence as soon as the meaning of adoption began to set in. Already as a preschooler she realized that some aspects of her personality reflected her adoptive family while others originated with her birthfamily (Gritter, 1989, p. 13). Decades later she observes, "I'm at home in a variety of situations," and her comment rings true. Sure-footed and fully identified with her adoptive family, she is also at home on campus, in church, with birthrelatives, with in-laws, and with various sets of friends. Sara knows there is hazard in thinking too broadly about home, for if one is at home everywhere, perhaps one is not fully at home anywhere. She understands that there is an element of exclusive intimacy about one's home, but this is not a dimension she chooses to emphasize. For Sara, home is an inclusive concept. It is a state of mind and heart that makes room for all the people she loves and counts on.

Sara's homey integration of formative factors is akin to what theologian Volf calls a "catholic personality." He explains,

> A catholic personality is a personality enriched by otherness, a personality which is what it is only because multiple others have been reflected in it in a particular way. ...The Spirit unlatches the doors of my heart saying: "You are not only you; others belong to you too." (1996, p. 51)

With its generous view of affiliation, hospitality holds the potential to ease the loyalty pressures that afflicted earlier generations of adoptive persons. Making sense of the totality of one's adoption will always be a daunting task, but the unencumbered opportunity to explore and acknowledge all influences makes the project of integration more workable. By countering adoption's undercurrent of separation with a vivid spirit of welcome, hospitality throws open the doors of multidimensional at-homeness. On these terms, an adoptive person's embrace of one branch of family no longer carries the risk of alienating the others.

The hospitable home is naturally inclusive. Gracious adoptive families say an enthusiastic "Yes!" to the fullness of their children, and they are humble about the extent of their influence. They set up a big tent that makes room for and honors many contributors, and gracious birthfamilies do the same thing. Building on the bedrock of an unconditional acceptance and a steadfast commitment, the heartfelt message of these hospitious parents is that differences are welcome, we don't have to be identical to belong to each other. Our commonalities are sweet, but our differences enrich our repertoire of possibilities and expand our connection to the community around us. The hospitable home welcomes and celebrates the wholeness of the adoptive person. Embraced as an insider by a robust and diverse cast of influential characters, the adoptive person is positioned to feel authentically at home in the world. This peace of mind and soul is the sumptuous fruit of genuine, hospitious acceptance.

CHAPTER 6

NATAL HOSPITALITY:
The Art of Gentle Transition

The idea that it is best to swiftly separate mothers and their slated-for-adoption newborns has long held sway in the field of infant adoption. A threefold case is made for this practice. First, a speedy shift in care is thought to spare prospective birthparents the emotional pain that accompanies intimate interaction with the baby they may be parting with. Second, it provides immediate clarity and consistency of care for the baby, thereby presumably reducing her prospects for confusion. With only one set of caregivers to get used to, the thinking goes, the newborn quickly attaches to her new parents. Third, adoptive parents are delighted to welcome the much-anticipated baby into their home and hearts at the earliest possible moment. It appears, then, that the swift transition serves the interests of all the major participants. Additionally, although our preferences are of secondary importance, practitioners routinely endorse a speedy transfer of responsibility because it shortens the time of uncertainty, the phase when anxious clients ask the most of us. Supported from many angles, the practice is thoroughly entrenched and seldom questioned.

With so many changes in adoption taking hold in recent years, perhaps it is time to take a fresh look at this practice. Given the bent of this book, the pressing question is, how does the practice of swift transition look when held up to the light of hospitality?

I first wondered about the transitional process when I was new to the field and read Linda Cannon Burgess's *The Art of Adoption*. In that book, published in the mid 1970's, this wise and seasoned social worker observed,

> ...As a medical social worker...I witnessed the heart-breaking separation of unmarried mothers from their new-born infants as their babies were removed by the adoption workers. ...I was especially struck by the timing of the sep-aration, which occurred two or three days after delivery when the mother's instinctive protectiveness of her infant was at its peak. It seemed barbaric. (1976, p. ii)

Even as a novice, I reacted to the word "barbaric," a word suggesting that the practice was not exactly bathed with hospitality.

As my work in adoption continued, every now and then a particularly mature prospective birthmother—usually a strong proponent of breastfeeding—would come along and question prevailing practice. Frustrated by the abruptness of the process, these resolute women proposed unconventional plans calling for a gradual shift of care from themselves to the adoptive family. They nursed their babies and spent more time with them than other birthparents did. Clearly, they relished every moment of interaction with their children. While their communion with their babies was tinged with resignation and sadness, it was also noticeably peaceful and fulfilling.

My concern about the pace of transition accelerated as a result of simple but haunting comments made by two strong voices for children, Dr. Marcy Axness and Michael Trout. Each has uncommon ability to see the world through the eyes of babies and to report clearly on what they see, so their impressions are invaluable to those who place priority on the interests of children. With a handful of words, they call us to reconsider our transitional habits.

An adoptive person with a deep interest in pre- and perinatal dynamics, Axness is an unabashed advocate for the respectful treatment of children from their earliest moments. Reflecting on the speedy transition of responsibility from birthparents to adoptive parents, she observed, "We seem to think that if we execute the 'hand-off' quickly enough, maybe the baby won't notice" (letter to the author, September 9, 1995). When I first read her comment, I laughed out loud; the idea that we could fool a baby if we were sneaky enough set me to giggling. As my mirth subsided though, dismay set in. Is this the first lesson we want to teach adoptive children, that the important adults in their lives are inclined to play tricks on them, and that things are not always what they seem? Who is fooling whom? And exactly how stupid do we think babies are?

Trout is a pioneering infant mental health specialist with a gift for describing the interactions he observes in fresh and memorable terms. While addressing the issue of gentle transition at an open adoption conference, he matter-of-factly referred to the separation between the prospective birthmother and baby in stunning terms. He called the event the "first disruption," and it is fair to say that his choice of words significantly disrupted my professional comfort. *Disruption*, after all, is not a very happy word. At a minimum, it conveys uproar and confusion. For many of us it means something even more distressing, for in the world of adoption, *disruption* is an especially charged word that refers to the unraveling of an adoption because it has failed. It is among the worst of possibilities, and it is something adoption workers will go to great lengths to prevent. So, when he employs this potent word, Trout riles substantial professional angst and implicitly raises the indicting question, "Has everything possible been done to prevent this upsetting interruption in the usual course of events?" Moreover, in concocting the phrase "first disruption," he hints that precedent is set and that additional upheavals may lurk around the corner. His perception makes it clear that we can no longer treat the transition of care between families as benign, inconsequential events. As red-alert circumstances, they demand and deserve our best and most creative energy.

One last preliminary observation: When it comes to the adoption of older children, we have learned the importance of moving through the transition gradually, incremental step by incremental step. If this careful process makes sense for toddlers, why don't we operate in the same fashion for newborns? Do we really think it is best for the newborn who has just exchanged the comforts of the womb for the vagaries of "life outside" to abruptly lose everything familiar? Or does our eagerness to install the new parents belie our claim to serve first the needful child, and reveal systemic fear that prospective birth-parents might change their mind if given more time to think? It appears that the impetus to speedy transition is rooted in the desire to protect prospective adoptive parents from the specter of disap-pointment. If this impression is correct, our challenge is to find other ways to help these vulnerable would-be parents manage their anxiety, so the pace of transition can be better tailored to the needs of the baby.

I believe the transitional process can benefit from the application of hospitable principles. This shift in approach asks a great deal of the adults involved. To say the least, these vulnerable parties already have a lot going on—hospital protocols to contend with, decisions to make, papers to sign, and friends and family to keep posted. It is a bewildering circumstance, and even those who appear to find their way with relative ease report that the experience leaves them exhausted. Nevertheless, hospitality, with its guest-host framework and its emphasis on noticing the newcomer and listening to and making room for the person who feels out of place, offers some important insights.

Confusion is reduced when we recognize that the transitional project is hosted and organized by the potential birthparents. Labor and delivery is their event. Furthermore, they are the newborn's first voice, so for at least two good reasons, this is rightfully their scene to direct. Those who wish to assist them—family, friends, profes-sionals, and would-be adoptive parents—do well to make lots of room for them to move through this experience in the way they deem best, and then follow their lead. We do them no favor if we shepherd them onto conventional paths. Better that we encourage them to think outside the lines and help them discover a transitional process that is uniquely theirs. Better, too, that we encourage them to take seriously their responsibility to think and speak for the baby. Since clarity of purpose is important, these goals are most likely met when significant prior thought goes into them. That said, it is also important to remember that plans are subject to change. There will be aspects of transition that are invented on the fly, and these inventions translate into moments of uncertainty as the process is reconfigured. Given the multilayered and often spontaneous nature of transition, participants need to remain "loosely astute" and adjust as events unfold. It helps a little to at least remain clear about who makes the decisions.

Potential birthparents have lots of emotional work to do once the baby arrives. Surely they need to revisit their thinking about what is best for the baby because, among other things, she constitutes new and extraordinary information to take into account. Prior analysis was abstract, but this stretching, yawning, cooing baby is very, very tangible, and her presence stirs powerful emotions that ought not be overlooked. Soul-searching is in order, and that reflection will most likely require time and privacy. If, after that soulful contemplation, adoption still makes sense, the transfer of caregiving responsibility can begin. But before any of that reflection occurs, the birthfamily needs to greet the newcomer.

In the transitional process, as in every other circumstance, hospitality begins with noticing. If we are not inclined to notice and greet someone fresh to the planet, the personification of innocence, whom will we welcome? How sad that in many adoptive situations the pace of transition is so swift that the universally acclaimed miracle of a new life is hardly acknowledged. To make a grand entrance to no applause is to spiritually whither. We have focused so much on helping birthparents say good-bye that we sometimes forget that first they must say hello. The simple wisdom of hospitality reminds us that a thoughtful transitional process spares no effort to help the newborn feel at home in her new surroundings. Plainly stated, this innocent newcomer deserves a hearty welcome from her first family.

The baby's parents deserve whatever time they need to fully welcome this child. The form their welcome takes is idiosyncratic; there can be no overall prescription for the way it happens. One hopes the process is leisurely and tender, governed by the baby's needs, not the system's. In the fashion of new parents everywhere, they do well to take inventory, counting all the fingers and toes and cataloguing family traits that have found their way to this next generation. This affectionate examination leads to an important conclusion: She is one of us, and we are glad. It is good to deliberately breathe in the inimitable fragrance of this remarkable baby, and it is good to give voice to all the hopes and dreams attached to her. As is the case with all births, there can never be too many pictures taken to capture the excitement. It is an occasion to document extravagantly with every imaginable combination of celebrants being preserved for later review. No matter the outcome, adoption or otherwise, the youngster will look back and take pleasure in the fact that her family greeted her and celebrated her arrival.

If the decision is to move forward with adoption[1], the baby's first parents do well to have a heart-to-heart talk with her. For their own clarity of mind, it is good for them to put their rationale into words, but even more to the point, the baby deserves an explanation. With big changes in her life course imminent, it only seems fair to reassure her and prepare her for the coming hours and days. Words are important, but tactile, hands-on care is even more powerful. Foremost among tactile reassurances is the opportunity to gain sustenance and immunity at the breast.

Transition and entrustment is like a second round of labor and delivery for the birthparents, only this time the work is almost entirely emotional, and the squirming, breathing outcome of the effort is a new set of relationships. Transition begins when birthparents consciously make room for the prospective adoptive parents and invite them to minister to the baby *as parents*. Their interaction with the baby may look much the same as it did when they first clucked and fawned as well-wishers, but the feel of it is entirely different once

---

[1] This refers to the cognitive and emotional decision. The actual moment of final decision will vary according to the provisions of the law and practices of the service provider. We must keep in mind that, until the true point of no return is reached, parents considering adoption for their children have a right to change their mind.

they have the first family's renewed endorsement as parents. This tipping point in the care of the baby launches a course that dramatically rearranges many lives. Shifting emotional gears, the birthparents move from the yin of welcome to the yang of farewell. Transition asks an odd good-bye of contemporary birthparents, not the all-encompassing, permanent good-bye that formerly characterized adoption, but one that signals a major change in authority and role. This transfer of responsibility translates into a diminution of their physical interaction with the baby, but it does not reduce their goodwill and love.

The hospitable perspective reminds us that participants need to respect each other throughout this emotional process. Decency requires this of us. But at the same time, it is important to recognize that respect for the needs of others need not come at the expense of one's own. There are moments when each participant needs to prioritize her own needs and hold the needs and wishes of the others in abeyance. Our shared commitment to creating an optimal life for the baby does not mean that we have to do everything together; some of the emotional work that prospective parents, birth or adoptive, need to do is best done apart. For the birthfamily, the time in the hospital—the time between the arrival of the baby and her moving on—is rich with sensations. She is all theirs in a way that soon passes, and these early hours brim with opportunity that, if lost, cannot be recovered. While it is remarkably gracious for them to involve the chosen family in these intimate moments, their generosity ought not cost them any of their exclusive time with the baby.

The transitional process feels like labor and delivery for the receiving family as well. They have a lot to handle as they read the cues of the new parents; attend to the needs of the baby to the extent they are welcomed; and manage their own diverse emotions. This is the hard work they do to emotionally connect to the baby, and the difficulty and intensity of the effort mysteriously adds to their appreciation and eventually to their sense of entitlement to her. Complicating these emotions are pangs of infertility that, even when they have long been dormant, may be stirred by this close brush with birth. Faced with the need to find their way through a high-stakes circumstance that is largely unscripted and over which they have no control, their emotional circuits approach an overload.

As guests, prospective adoptive parents greet and celebrate the baby's arrival on two levels. When they first greet her, it is as friends of the birthparents and as representatives of humankind, not as her new parents. They are there to support the first family. Later, only after the birthparents have clearly signaled that they want the prospective adoptive parents to step into the caregiving role, they greet the child as a potential member of their family. Although these layers of welcome are sometimes subtle, it is important that the nature of their welcome corresponds to the degree of endorsement the birthparents have granted.

There are times when hospitality means stepping forward, and times when it requires stepping back. The more difficult path is the stepping back. An arrangement involving outstanding prospective adoptive parents and an unhurried mother illustrates its difficulty. Timothy and Kathy Young "get" open adoption as well as any couple ever to go through our program—to a home study question asking how birthparents fit into open adoption, Kathy memorably answered, "That's like asking how John Lennon fit with the Beatles." It is difficult to imagine a family more understanding and supportive of birthparents. Danielle, the expectant mother who selected them with three months remaining in her pregnancy, knew she had lined up a treasure, yet, wanting to keep all of her options open, kept some emotional distance from them as she prepared for birth. Although the Youngs were eager to get to know her better, they respected her handling of the situation and provided the emotional space she desired.

The birth went well, but the newborn boy's stay in the hospital was protracted as a result of jaundice. The parents wanted Timothy and Kathy at the hospital in a generally supportive way, but, insofar as they were thoroughly enjoying their interaction with the baby, they were not inclined to include them in his care until he neared the time of discharge from the hospital. Intellectually, Kathy supported their handling of the circumstance, but on an emotional level, it bothered her. Physically, emotionally, and spiritually, she was gearing up to enter the maternal role and carry it out with all her considerable energy and love. As the hours and days went by, however, the opportunity was not offered to her, and this extraordinary woman, simultaneously supportive of Danielle's savoring of the baby and impatient for the unbridled opportunity to immerse this beguiling child in her love, grew frustrated. Recognizing that her frustration might grow into resentment, she did the only thing she could think of: she stepped back. Confident that the baby was receiving abundant love and attention, she stayed away from the hospital until the moment arrived when she was explicitly invited to step fully into the caregiving role. She knew there was a chance her retreat might be misunderstood by the first parents, but her hospitious instinct told her it was best to step back and make ample room for them to enjoy the baby. Birthparent advocate that she was and is, she knew her impatience would crowd the first parents if she stayed on the scene.

At almost the same time the Youngs were exercising hospitality in the form of stepping back, in a nearby hospital the Slaters were discovering that hospitality sometimes means precipitously stepping forward. They had been schooled by their social worker, who was in the process of writing a chapter about hospitious transition, to avoid presumptiveness in the hospital, and that the most respectful course was to give the mother who had selected them ample time and space to enjoy the baby. The advice made sense to them on at least three levels. First, they wanted the baby boy to be fully celebrated, and they wanted his welcome to be relaxed, dignified, and unhurried. Second, they held their new friend Katy in high regard and wanted her to thoroughly enjoy the wonders of this amazing child. Third, they considered a conservative approach to be in their own best interest. By celebrating the arrival of this new life as "Katy's Baby" rather than as "The Baby Who May Soon Be Ours," they were guarding as best they could their own psyches. It was a sensible approach, but it was not aligned with Katy's wishes. Her clear preference was to forthrightly install them as the baby's primary caregivers while carving out a supportive role for herself. Katy's signals to the Slaters were unmistakable: Adoption still makes sense, and I want you to report for parental duty immediately. For the Slaters, then, the hospitable path was to adjust their mindset and bring leadership to the situation sooner than expected.

The hospitable path is difficult to discover and travel, and the courage of those who find and follow it is seldom adequately recognized or appreciated. Their respectful deference quietly preserves adoption as a viable alternative for women and couples tackling untimely pregnancies. Fortunately, those who meander the hospitious path often find their own rewards. As one expectant adoptive mother whispered over the phone as she sat bedside keeping company with the intimate tangle of sleeping mother and baby, "*This is a beautiful thing.*"

That image of contented motherhood reminds us that the process of transition is more than an anxious time for everyone to somehow get through. The way the transition occurs becomes a metaphor for the entire experience. An adoptive mother supports this assertion with a story. She reports that they regularly tell the birth story of each of their children because the youngsters delight in the telling of these tales. She recalls patiently explaining to her 6-year-old how his little brother had joined the family. "We were there when Sam was born. Oh, what an exciting time that was! We spent lots of time in the hospital with him and with Carol [his birthmother]. Then, after a couple of amazing days, we took him home." Her son listened attentively, but did not say much at the time. A couple of weeks later, though, putting an unexpected spin on a particular word, he suddenly and indignantly asked, "Why did you *take* Sam from Carol?" He was bothered by the earlier rendition of the story because its phrasing did not make it unambiguously clear that the plan was fully endorsed by Sam's birthmother. The way the transition was handled was of great importance to him. If adoption was about *taking* children, he did not think well of the idea.

So how does it work? Exactly how is this event carried out? Do adoptive parents indeed *take* the baby, or do they *receive* her? Do birthparents *surrender* the baby and *walk away* from their responsibility, or do they *entrust* her to competent and loving arms? Is it a face-to-face, person-to-person moment of gutsy intimacy, or is it mediated and institutional? Is it a fully human, soulful experience, or is it businesslike? Does the baby drop out of one book and suddenly show up in another, or is one continuous story being written?

Ideally, everything we intend for the adoption long-term—honesty, tenderness, child-centeredness, humor, flexibility, mutual respect, and cooperation, to mention a few of the usual aspirations—will characterize the transition process. It is an opportunity to bring our values to life. If the child's interests are foremost from the beginning, valuable precedent is set. If we are playful and brave and bump through the tension and awkwardness of transition shoulder to shoulder, chances are we may sustain that mutually supportive style over the long haul.

One of the factors that complicates the transitional process is the suddenness of the hospital discharge. When the mother and baby are in good health, the hospital is eager for them to move on. The hospital discharge is a juncture that pointedly raises the question "What's next?" The usual answer suggests it is time for the families to go their separate directions, but that is not the only available course. The transitional process does not have to shrink into a transitional moment because the hospital says it is time to leave. The needs of the participants are not necessarily in sync with the needs of the institution, so there is no compelling reason for the momentous experience of transition to follow its time frame.

In recent years we have extended the time for transition by encouraging plans in which the baby is discharged from the hospital to the birthmother and then having the families move on to some predetermined familiar territory where they can let their hair down. In this safe place they can reflect on all they have been through and contemplate the future. Away from the hospital, they are free to put their own imprint on this time together, a time like none they have ever known. There are no gawkers or distractions; the only people present are those who love this child and who have chosen to work together. With the baby holding center stage, it is time to take inventory. Have we said all that we need to say, and have we done all that we need to do? Have we served this child well so far? It is in this intimate context that, when everyone is ready, one mother entrusts the baby into the arms of another.

Lisa and Daryl Bluhm and Josie, the wise-before-her-time mother who entrusted her baby to their care, handled their transition along the lines just described. After spending ample time in the hospital celebrating the baby's arrival, they left the hospital together. Josie and the baby piled into the Bluhms' car, and all of them made the half-hour journey to the Bluhms' home together. Josie's mother and sisters followed in another car. Once they arrived, they spent a couple of hours reviewing the amazing events of the prior months. It was a rich time of sharing, a much less nervous time than outsiders might presume. Away, at last, from the hospital and its institutional constraints, they were safe with each other. No one was pretending; no one was putting on a show. When Josie felt that the baby was, in her words, "safely snuggled into her new home," she knew it was okay to leave. It was not an easy ride home for her, but it was bearable because the moment of entrustment glowed with dignity and love and because she was surrounded with the love of her family.

With a twinkle in her eye, Sharon Roszia, quite possibly open adoption's wisest proponent, draws on recent advances in neuroscience and notes that babies come into this world "half baked." Since babies need some time to let their biology unfold and to get their bearings, she worries about "the demands that are made on both birthfamilies and adoptive families to 'get on with it.'" These pressures are woven into the fabric of the system, and they are difficult to counter. Roszia suggests that we do not have to think of parenting in serial terms. "I've become more and more a believer that in all possible ways it would be wonderful to have overlapping parents. The parents need to spend some time alone with the baby and make sure this [adoption] is what they want to do, and then make sure there's some real overlapping time so that the baby has a real chance to transfer attachments" (Roszia, Interview 2004).

Participants who are attracted to this approach will find ways to extend their time together. They might, for example, negotiate with the physician for extra time in the hospital, or they might make arrangements for the mother to stay with the adoptive family for a while. If that is not workable, they may arrange for a round of meaningful daily visits. Others may escape to a cottage or cabin for a spell. Holed up as "overlapping parents," the families can idle some time away, talking, praying, laughing, cooking, and taking turns attending to the baby. Gloriously, there is nothing for them to be in a hurry about. The extra time enables the adults to get to know each other better and enrich their capacity to read each other. More importantly, it gives the baby a chance to get used to all of them.

Hospitality challenges our thinking that the process of transition is something to get through as quickly as possible. It invites us to slow down and savor a formative time in the life of a beloved child. It asks us to fully notice the newcomer as she is, not as we might like her to be. When we approach the situation with the spirit of hospitality, we recognize that the baby enters this world with a past, and we do our best to honor that history and build on it. The fashioning of an integrated life is the existential task for every adoptive person, but how does she go about this if her story begins with dis-integration? Transitional hospitality seeks to create a beginning that holds up well as the story moves forward.

We have a lot to learn about all this, especially about the needs of the neonate. As our knowledge grows, so, if we are to adjust our practices accordingly, must our resolve and courage, for it is not easy to change longstanding habits. To make transition plans more baby-centered, we need to work harder than ever to take into account the capabilities of everyone involved. Recognizing that what works gloriously for one set of families may be torture for another, we do well to hospitably craft individualized plans. Whatever form our plans take, they need to shine with courage and cooperation because they set the tone for all that follows.

CHAPTER 7

INVERTED HOSPITALITY:
Working Through a Change of Heart

"I have two questions," the would-be adoptive father hollered as he crossed the parking lot to approach the mother of the child he had hoped to adopt. They were meeting at a grocery store located halfway between their homes, and the purpose of the meeting was to return the baby to his mother. The entrustment that had occurred eight hours earlier was to be inverted; now the baby would go from his arms to hers. No one had predicted this turn of events, but, upon returning home after her discharge from the hospital, the empty-armed mother began vomiting. Retching without relief for hours, she literally feared for her life. Although her heart broke for the prospective adoptive parents whom she had come to love, she saw no alternative but to ask for her baby's return. She made the necessary calls, and now the awkward moment of undoing had arrived.

Having closed the distance between them so he could lower his voice, the man who wanted with all his heart to be a father softly asked, "Do you still love us? I hope so, because we still love you! And another thing. Do you promise that when this young fellow grows up to be President some day you will give us eight hours of credit?" The tension of the moment vanished, chased off by the goodwill that had characterized all of their earlier interactions and which was still in effect. Yes, double yes; she still loved them, and, of course, she would be sure they got all the credit they deserved. The connection they forged prenatally had taken root, and their relationship now took on meaning that went beyond the possibility of adoption. She asked them to be the baby's godparents, and they ended up babysitting for each other when the couple subsequently adopted other children.

For those who have eyes to see it, there is much that is beautiful in the realm of open adoption. Sometimes it is seen in those conspicuously joyous occasions when participants literally celebrate their coming together with fireworks. Other times it is evident in simple moments of thoughtfulness—the small gesture of recognition and remembrance. Oddly enough, it is often most clear in moments of confusion and anguish, including those times when parents experience a change of heart and set aside their plan for adoption.

What possible sense does it make to introduce what many regard as open adoption's greatest horror, the birthparent change of heart, in the context of beauty? I do this because in a surprising way, these situations strike me as some of our program's most impressive moments. Surely everything is magnified in these dramatic circumstances—the sadness, the awkwardness, the anger, *and* the strength of character. These situations have the potential for beauty because they are so primal. Prior to the change of heart, it is possible for the prospective adoptive parents—required by fate, it seems, to woo the favor of potential birthparents—to present an accommodating, amiable image, but pretense cannot hold up in the face of freshly altered intentions. Everything artificial, everything ulterior, is stripped away, and we are afforded an opportunity to discover the soul of these folks now that there is no payoff for friendly behavior. When, in the face of demolished hope, prospective adoptive parents find a way to respond with poise, they embody grace. When some raw part of them wants to lash out with frustration, but they instead respond with tenderness, it is a holy moment.

Perhaps this reminder that there is potential beauty even in this very difficult aspect of adoptive practice helps us to frame the subject of changed intentions in more positive terms than we might have otherwise. We need this reminder because we are often so grim about this prospect. Our language turns apocalyptic. The change of heart scenario looms so frightening, in fact, that numbers of would-be adoptive families travel around the world and brave an assortment of international anxieties to avoid this possibility. While I do not want to suggest that reversed intentions are always beautiful any more than I would suggest that every adoption that goes forward is satisfactory, I do wish to offer the hope that we can consider these situations without prejudice. If there is any junction in the adoption journey that can benefit from the grace of hospitality, it is that of the change of heart.

Dave Forton, the adoptive father whose story launched this chapter, was able to handle his disappointment with grace for two reasons: He was very clear in his thinking about the venture he was undertaking, and he is a natural master of hospitality. As much as he wanted to open his life to a child, he did not let his burgeoning love for the baby overwhelm his understanding of the process, nor did he let it subvert his determination to respectfully interact with the baby's family. He and his wife, Sandy, were clear-headed about the uncertainties of the process and clear-hearted about the way they would play their part. They tackled adoption the way they approach other challenges—heads up and with concern for others.

The Fortons did not see themselves as victims when their new friend changed her mind. Although her decision was unexpected, it did not really surprise them. After all, people change their mind about all sorts of things every day, sometimes several times in the same day. They also knew full well that there is nothing on earth to match the bond between mother and child, so it was hardly a shock when this loving woman they had come to know decided to resume her maternal role. The gravity of the prior planning meant little once the baby arrived; no matter how firm the expectant mother's prenatal intentions, they understood that the surprising outcome is always adoption. What is more, the Fortons did not expose themselves to this emotional risk lightly. They had weighed the advantages and disadvantages carefully before entering the experience and had concluded that the potential benefits were worth the evident risks. In order to provide an innocent baby a safe and loving start in life, they were willing to extend themselves in ways that exceed the ordinary.

Sensible, realistic thinking was an important element in the Fortons' composure. Their firm grasp of the facts kept them from being swept away with presumption. They were clear that he was not their child to raise until his mother made a final decision to that effect. Even more important than their clear-headedness, though, was their robust spirit of hospitality. Certainly they hoped to bring a child into the family, but it was also important to them that the baby's mother came through the journey intact. Truth be known, they were never very nervous about the experience. Each step in the process pleased them, and they found their relationship with the prospective birthmother lively and meaningful. The joy of having been chosen, hearing the prenatal heartbeat, and being included in the experience of birth were amazing gifts in their own right, and they were appreciative. The opportunity to get to know the baby's mother was its own reward, and they knew that no matter the outcome, they were going to be okay as long as their connection to her was authentic.

The Fortons approached the prospect of adoption with all of the hallmarks of hospitality. They embodied goodwill, respect, and courage, and their interactions featured the skills of noticing, listening, and making room. As a consequence, freed of the burden of self-preoccupation, the Fortons journeyed with far less anxiety than most of their peers. They illustrate the paradoxical power of hospitality: They were protected from anxiety by taking the risks of hospitality. By tempering their self-concern with concern for others, they became less vulnerable. Their anxiety was relieved in proportion to their appreciation of the first family. Hospitality did not protect them from loss, but it did spare them the character-altering effects of fear.

This is a good time to distinguish between authentic hospitality and pseudo-hospitality. Nouwen advises that hospitality requires that we reveal ourselves. "When we want to be really hospitable we not only have to receive strangers but also to confront them by an

unambiguous presence, not hiding ourselves behind neutrality. ...
No real dialogue is possible between somebody and a nobody" (1975,
p. 70). We are easier to relate to when we are clear about our values
and intentions. If "hospitality" takes the form of self-abnegation, a
sort of doormat rendition of care and concern that attends to the
other at the expense of one's self, it does not ring true. This counterfeit offers a hollow gift, for there is no self on hand to carry out a
relationship over time. Healthy hospitality does not elevate the other
over one's self; it views him as an equal. There are phases when more
is asked of one party or the other, but over time hospitality will
strengthen everyone involved. No one, neither provider nor receiver,
will be diminished.

To no one's surprise, most prospective adoptive parents initially
approach adoption unapologetically single-minded. Their goal is to
add a child to their family, nothing more and nothing less, and the
success or failure of their effort is gauged accordingly. Had this been
the Fortons' view of adoption, their cohort's change of course would
have left them defeated. For hospitality-minded adoptive parents,
however, there is more to the agenda; their journey is multi-dimen-
sional. While they surely seek a positive outcome for themselves, they
are also sincerely concerned that the other family moves toward a constructive outcome. For these folks with a larger view, success or failure takes into account more than whether an adoption moves forward.

Going into a change of heart scenario, one hopes, for everyone's
sake, the parties are situated in a deeply hospitable context. As they
strive to dispense grace in one of adoption's most stressful circumstances, they stand in need of it themselves.

The stage for hospitable interaction between adoptive participants is set early on by the professionals involved. As stated in this
book's Introduction, the task of the professional is to "create a context in which remarkable things can happen." We serve participants
well when we offer a system that welcomes, respects, equips, and supports them. In that kind of setting, they can operate from strength.
The preparation and support we offer does not in itself produce
excellence; it simply improves the likelihood that the excellence

within participants will emerge as they take each other into account in anxious circumstances.

It is not enough for adoption hopefuls to cross their fingers and hope for the best. As part of their effort to prepare for adoption, families need to seriously consider the possibility that plans might abruptly change. Their intellectual grasp of the rationale for taking on the risks inherent in the situation must be unshakable, because that bit of readiness is the easy part. Emotional preparation is more difficult if not impossible, for how does one find emotional protection in a situation like this? Babies stir primal emotions, and no one will be spared. With more thought, it occurs to us that no one actually wants to be "protected" from the wonder of a baby. All participants can do is draw on their faith and make sure that their support people—both generic and adoption-specific—are well informed and readily available. As they weather a season of heightened vulnerability, their challenge is to accept the loving hospitality of those who are there for them.

Adoptive mother Heidi Grebe made a conscious effort to prepare for the possibility of a change of heart as soon as they welcomed on a temporary basis the son who eventually became a permanent member of their family. Recognizing that that outcome would be hard on everyone involved, including the baby's mother, she painstakingly rehearsed for the possibility by imagining the time and place of the meeting to return the baby to his mother and practicing words of grace that might bring dignity to such an awkward situation. As it turned out, the moment never came, but she knew it could have, and she was as realistic and ready as anyone could be.

The prospect of a change of heart merits discussion even—or should we say, especially—in those circumstances where expectant parents do not want to think about the possibility. The discussion is not meant to undermine their resolve toward adoption; it is a matter of keeping options alive and being ready for as many of the potential outcomes as we can reasonably imagine. In a calm moment, impressions about the best ways to handle a change of heart are shared. Even if the adoption moves forward exactly as planned, this is an important conversation because sooner or later an unexpected twist will arise, and it will be easier to manage because of the earlier effort to anticipate the upset and confusion.

It is not easy to travel the adoption trail alone. Worry greedily consumes emotional energy, and knowledgeable encouragement is often hard to find. A hospitable system brings people of common purpose together and in doing so, offers the comfort of companionship. These connections are heartening, for those who set out to do adoption with concern for the others involved invariably encounter doubters along the way. Detractors chip away with knowing sighs and forthright skepticism. They are persistent, and their carping takes a toll. Against that backdrop, it is encouraging to spend time with others who "get it." Sharing a commitment to what they consider an honorable form of adoption, peers learn from each other and inspire each other with examples of courageous decency. They are there for each other in an especially helpful way when setbacks occur, a way that contains not a hint of "I told you so" or "What were you thinking?" To the contrary, hospitious peers express admiration for their efforts to live out their convictions.

When parents who considered adoption seriously enough to invite potential adoptive parents into the journey change course, we expect them to treat the would-be adoptive parents hospitably. The most important thing is honesty. It is challenge enough for prospective adoptive families to handle a change of heart when they are well informed, and it is substantially more difficult to handle if they feel misled. If at any point the first family has misgivings about moving ahead with the contemplated adoption, the merciful course is to keep the prospective adoptive family informed, even when it is obvious that doubt is not what the hope-filled family wants to hear. A straightforward explanation helps. In our experience, a change of heart seldom has anything to do with the behavior of the prospective adoptive parents. Knowing that they did not mess up does not change the outcome for the would-be parents, but it at least spares them rounds of self-recrimination.

The professionals overseeing the process contribute greatly as facilitators, but, as was true when the plan was adoption, it is best when the communication between the families is direct. The last thing anybody wants in the middle of an emotional transition is miscommunication. This direct approach asks a lot of the parents who changed their course. They feel like assassins and understandably want to avoid the carnage, but experience indicates that personal explanations produce the best outcomes. If they handle this turn of events hospitably—with goodwill, respect, and courage—they will be freed up to unreservedly rejoice in their resumption of parental duty. If, on the other hand, they dodge the difficult moment and leave it in the hands of the professional, everyone exits with a sense of unfinished business.

Once the news that there will not be an adoption has been delivered, it is usually best to carry out the inverted entrustment without delay. In most instances, this serves the baby well and suits the wishes of both families. The first family is eager to resume their provision of care and the crestfallen would-be adoptive family typically finds their continued interaction with the baby emotionally excruciating. The baby is sure to pick up on their distress. There is little reason to dally, yet it is important to proceed with dignity. For the sake of the adults, it is good to review all that they have gone through together and ponder their remarkable shared journey. It is good to wish each other all the best and disengage graciously. For the baby's sake, it is important that the reactivated parents be informed of all that has been learned about his routines. If the baby was apart from his first family for an extended period of time, it may be necessary to move incrementally so the transition is not abrupt. Once again he needs time and permission to adjust, and the idea of caring for him as overlapping parents merits consideration if the adults are capable of it.

When prospective adoptive parents encounter a change of course, they are plunged into loss and grief. Finding their way through that profound disappointment is hard work. My reflex as a professional is to flee the powerlessness and sadness of these would-be parents, who are in shock over their shredded hopes. As we process their loss we will surely unearth their anger, and I am never eager to step onto the shooting range. My reticence has foundation, too, for I know, since it is impossible to sufficiently prepare participants for these turn-abouts, that they will stand on righteous ground as they express their frustration. It is difficult, too, because there is no problem solving to be done; there is no remedy at hand to relieve their aching empti-ness. There is little I can do apart from standing alongside as they sift though their experience and review its twists and turns. All one can do is show up. We were with them in the pleasing stretches of the journey, and hospitality compels us to be there in harder times to offer a bit of understanding and respect. It seems paltry, but it matters.

These situations are not all alike. Some are more unexpected than others, and, in truth, some are easier to come to terms with than oth-ers. Reaction to a change of heart varies according to the extent of the relationship between the families, the baby's prospects for a love-filled life, and the would-be adoptive family's prospects for new opportunities to adopt. The most difficult of these circumstances are those where there is concern about the baby's safety and well-being. In those situations, the heaviness of grief is compounded by the burden of worry.

In our retrospective analysis of the change of heart experience, we are reminded of our dependence on others. None of us has con-trol in these adoptive adventures. All we can do is move through them in a transparent, honest, and respectful manner. Would-be adoptive parents are not consoled when the people around them minimize the loss they have endured. They may handle the change of heart experience with remarkable grace, but we know the empty place in their heart is gaping and raw. At some point, after sufficient time goes by and healing begins, they will likely discover bits of sil-ver lining. Shaking their heads with amazement at what they are about to say, families often comment that despite the pain of the experience, it had taught them a lot. It is a somber version of what many families say earlier when the outcome is still undetermined: that no matter how the adoption turns out, they were living the most amazing days of their lives. They were chosen, they were trusted, and they were in on the miracle of new life. They met new and interesting people, and they gained valuable experience that will serve them well in subsequent adoption forays. They did their best in a difficult circumstance, and their self-respect stayed intact. With time and healing, they will find hope for another day.

CHAPTER 8

DOING HOSPITALITY:
Working with Differences

The call to the adoptive family came in around 11 o'clock in the evening, not the most promising time of day for the phone to ring. It was the birthmother of one of their children, and she had news for the family. "I'm pregnant, I'm getting married in six weeks, and I want all four of you in the wedding. I want Sally to be the flower girl, Mark to be the ring bearer. I want you to be my maid of honor, and Charlie wants Tom to be his best man. What do you think? Isn't it great?" The adoptive mother caught her breath, mumbled congratulations, and encouraged further thought.

There was, in fact, plenty to think about. The adoptive mother climbed into bed and began telling her groggy husband about the call she had just handled. "Wait a minute before you say any more," he interrupted. "First tell me, am I awake, or am I still sleeping?" He wasn't sure because the details drifting through his brain struck him as something straight from the realm of restless sleep: *Best man? Did we hit it off that well when we met that one time?* For several reasons, the proposed marriage did not strike them as particularly promising. Carol's divorce from her first husband had just come through, and Charlie was simply the latest fellow to catch her attention. He had not been in her life very long, and his employment history was checkered at best. In a nutshell, they worried that going along with Carol's request would enable her unrealistic, short-ranged thinking and reduce her chances of someday settling into a stable lifestyle. Marriage is important to them, and it pained them to see it approached this lightly. On the other hand, the request was moving testimony to Carol's regard for them. Although it was a struggle for her to meet the demands of everyday living, not to mention the pressures of a committed relationship, why, they asked themselves, should she have to go through life alone? "Who are we to judge," the designated maid of honor asked her husband, shaking her head, "who are we to judge?"

It is one thing to talk about hospitality and another to do it. When it comes to *doing* hospitality, the challenge is in the handling of differences. Most of us do pretty well at making room for people who are like us, but we grow faint-hearted when we encounter people with dissimilar values and lifestyles. Coming to terms with those we consider "different" is the hard work of hospitality.

Before we discuss differences, we do well to consider similarities. Frankly stated, adoption is simpler when the families involved have a lot in common. An easy way to illustrate this is to conceptualize adoption as a form of transplantation. Conscientious gardeners do their best to keep the soil and climate of the source and the destination as similar as possible when they uproot and replant seedlings. This is the logic of matching, long one of adoption's most daunting duties. Congruence between birth- and adoptive families is desired because it asks fewer adjustments of everyone involved, most importantly the children. Whether they are aware of it or not, most potential birthparents look for commonality as they assess and select prospective adoptive parents for their children. Similarity reduces anxiety in adoption, but as much as we long for it, there are many situations where little is available.

Families sharing the experience of adoption may differ in their personalities and socio-economic standing. They may be dissimilar in race, religion, values, lifestyle, and favorite sports teams. Surely some of these variables are more defining and exclusive than others, but they all affect their prospects for connection and mutuality. We could test compatibility combinations for the rest of our days. Are prospects for a satisfying adoption better, for example, for a pairing of rich Presbyterians and poor Presbyterians, or for rich Presbyterians and rich atheists? Who could possibly know? This difficulty is not a reason to abandon efforts to link similar families, but it does drive us to acknowledge the elusive nature of compatibility. As appealing as it may be to try to engineer similarity between families, experience teaches that efforts to help participants handle their differences will bear greater fruit.

For many reasons, this is challenging work. Since it takes courage, energy, and skill to tackle our differences, it is tempting to minimize or ignore them. Participants and professionals find it easy to co-dependently overlook the obvious in their eagerness to keep things moving forward. Further, differences arise in many forms. Some are trivial while others appear life-threatening. Understandably, then, we react to them unevenly. While some generate delight, others stir abhorrence. Between these extremes are gradations of approval, neutrality, and forbearance.

It is also clear that we vary in our ability and willingness to work with differences. Some people appear to have little aptitude for this effort, and some of those who do have the capacity are not inclined to do the work. This disconnect in capacity and willingness is a challenge for adoption professionals. Families with little capacity or interest in working with differences may be exemplary in many ways, but their suitability for adoption is suspect. If we believe that an adopted child will fare best in circumstances where her families are mutually respectful, we need adoptive families who are willing and able to constructively tackle dissimilarities. To move forward with adoption when there is little prospect for respect between the families is to create a circumstance in which the child will have a difficult time settling in and finding acceptance. If a we/they split exists between the birth- and adoptive families, it will soon exist in the heart of the adoptive child as well.

One more preliminary thought about differences. From whose vantage point shall we approach this subject? This discussion will mostly focus on the differences between adoptive parents and birthparents because their relationship cradles all others, but we must remember that there are other differences that call for attention. It is a startling moment, for instance, when the awareness suddenly hits a parent, birth or adoptive, "I don't get this kid. She is a stranger to me." And it is at least as disconcerting for a child, reflecting on her various parents, to realize in a deep way, "I am not like them."

Those are cold words. They send a shiver through the adoptive community. What are we to do with this visceral sensation of not being like each other? Answers do not come easily, but some relief is found through the application of hospitality. Hospitality does not alter the fact that we are different, but it can mitigate the alienation that so often accompanies a finding of difference. Hospitality offers a path to understanding and connection.

Naturally hospitable people notice the discomforts generated by differences and reflexively go to them. They cannot help but minister to these anxieties. The rest of us view these points of conflict uneasily; our reflex is to give them wide berth. The hospitality we offer is more self-conscious and deliberative, something we gear up for. This next section explores this gearing-up process. The discussion is not meant as a script or formula for hospitality, for none exists. A range of possibilities is presented in the hope that those who set out to hospitate will find a workable idea or two.

Hospitious Motives

Conscious hospitality requires a compelling motive. We will not get very far in our efforts to connect to others unless we definitively answer the questions "Why are we doing this?" and "What are we trying to accomplish?" For hospitious participants, the answers are clear and convincing: We embark on these adoption adventures for the sake of children, and our goal is to create a truly promising circumstance for each child involved. Lacking clarity of purpose, we might have given up after only modest effort, having done that which was convenient but little more. Mindful that our investments benefit children, however, we doggedly inch forward with conviction. For the sake of children, we accept inconvenience as a fact of life. For the sake of a particular child, we commit to doing whatever it takes to surround her with maximum nurturing.

The truth of adoption is stark—*those "other people" are not optional.* In fact, not only are they not optional, they are important contributors to this child's story, and they always will be. It is best, then, to fully settle this issue in our minds and hearts. That means giving up our protest, martyrdom, and fantasies, along with all the psychological bargaining that we find so appealing. No more deliberation or equivocation; these diversions siphon off energy. When we love someone, we accept the entirety of that person and the fullness of her story. She would not be the amazing person she is apart from the entourage of players in her life.

Clarity about the purpose of the endeavor enables us to move into a "just do it" mode. Embracing difference is simply the way it is. On board and fully resolved, we are freed up to move ahead with all the honesty and candor and playfulness we can muster. No one can do much about how the others involved carry out their obligations— they may behave in ways that are surprisingly impressive or disappointing. All any of us can do is hold up our end of the arrangement and a little bit more.

Hospitious Preparation

Holding up my end calls for substantial self-awareness. I need to be aware of my quirks, fears, irrationalities, insecurities, and prejudices, and I need to keep these idiosyncrasies under control. There is a risk that I may project my failings onto the stranger. If that happens, the worries I hold regarding her are worries she might rightly hold about me! Self-awareness is especially important when it comes to fear. As much as we fear others for their deficiencies, their goodness may frighten us more, and we start to fret that they might someday surpass us in the eyes of the child. But how nonsensical is this line of thought? Should we live in fear of the goodness of others?

Also, I need to do my homework and improve my awareness of my journeymates. Is there some reading to be done, or a movie that offers insight into their psyche and circumstance? Are there people to talk to? Any spokespersons, experts or ordinary souls, who might advance my understanding? Of course we have to be careful about generalizing too broadly about any subgroup, but we honor those around us by making the effort to understand them better.

Hospitious Attitudes

A spirit of goodwill prompts us to focus on the best qualities of the other. We resist the temptation to exaggerate the ways she is different and reduce her to these differences. Father Pierre-François de Béthune comments, "Our brother is more of a stranger and mystery than we think, the stranger more of a brother than we think" (2002, p. 23). When we operate with goodwill, we look forward to learning about the breadth and depth of our compatriots' experiences.

Writer Brennan Manning makes a case for the importance of openness in our discussion of differences.

> Openness serves as a bridge to the world of others, to understand the thoughts of others, to feel what others are feeling. In other words, if we're open, we're able to enter the existential world of others even if at times we can't identify with someone's particular world. (2002, p. 113)

Openness disarms. It demonstrates interest and communicates to the other that she is valued. Slow to judge, a spirit of openness provokes few defenses.

Many of us fear that our encounters with people who are different will not go well. Out of our element, we fret that we may blunder and offend them, and we expect they may do the same. We fear the confusion of it all, the questions that will be unearthed, and the awkward circumstances we may encounter or worse yet, stir up and set into motion ourselves. We worry that our inadequacies will be exposed.

To tackle these fears, to leave our comfortable ways and encounter the mystery of the other, we need courage. It's not the burst of courage to lead a bayonet charge into hostile territory, but the puff of courage that enables us to ask someone we don't know very well, "Could you help me understand your view of this situation?" It is the bit of courage that enables us to quietly share our deepest thoughts and feelings in those moments when we suspect they may not play very well.

The attitudinal key to working with differences is humility. A doormat routine this is not. To the contrary, it is a form of robust honesty founded in the conviction that we all have important contributions to make. To be rooted in humility is to be at peace with our limits. It is to concede that I know too little about the other and her context to judge. My hunch is that she is handling things with at least as much grace as I would, were our circumstances inverted. Humility also compels me to admit that I have my hands full managing my own challenges and opportunities. When I engage others with a spirit of humility, I acknowledge that I have a lot to learn and that they have a lot to teach. In this frame of mind, I am more interested in changing my ways than in changing theirs.

Hospitious Perspectives

Effective hospitators are eager to learn. Brimming with curiosity about the differences they encounter, they resemble amateur anthropologists. Of course, they need to stay engaged, but some part of them remains constructively curious. "Now what are they up to?" wonders the keen observer. "How interesting. Why do they do these things, and why do they do them the way they do?" Assuming that most behaviors are in some way functional, they watch and listen intently in the hope of discovering new possibilities. Chances are the other family will reveal insights that might have been missed had their paths not crossed. In many ways, this opportunity to encounter new perspectives is the payoff for the sincerely hospitable.

Another hospitious perspective sees the encounter as an adventure. When we interact with ideas and experiences unlike our own, we rise above the tedium of the ordinary. A venture into unfamiliar territory is energizing. To succeed, we must concentrate and keep our wits about us. Instead of plodding down the same old paths long ago paved by others, we find ourselves blazing a trail, suddenly alert and pleasingly light-footed.

Yet another way to approach the nexus of different worlds is to view our compatriots as in-laws. This is an apt approach because the parallels between marriage and adoption are close and illuminating. Many of us have found a rich training ground in our in-laws. In-laws, like it or not, must contend with each other. We are each other's givens, stuck with each other for better or worse. At the very least, civility is required, but this coupling holds the potential for much warmer interaction.

Allow me a brief personal illustration: My parents-in-law hospitably gave my wife and me ample space and opportunity to find our way. Contrary to stock in-law humor, they kept their opinions to themselves, not badgering us with unsolicited advice or criticism. Simply stated, they had faith in us. No doubt we tested that faith regularly, but their confidence was steadfast. Their patience and grace provided us a foundation for growth. Their example is instructive. Outstanding in-laws take the view that those folks who are new to the family will probably be all right in the end despite their rough edges. The better course is to restrain the impulse to offer suggestions for improvement and give them plenty of opportunity to prove themselves. Patience may bring, I like to think, exponential dividends.

Hospitious Tasks

If goodwill exists, there are many ways for the consciously hospitable to put it into play. Consider several hospitious behaviors that may help adoptive participants get to know each other better:

- **Commit to honesty:** One of the most difficult things to do as we address differences is to speak the truth. It is often easier to look the other way and overlook our differences, but the easier way will not take us very far. In some instances "Let's just keep it light" conversation may lead to tolerance, but it seldom leads to enduring understanding or connection. Meaningful connection requires deeper honesty. When an especially wise and playful pair of mothers, birth and adoptive, were asked how they had built their remarkable relationship, they explained that they had made a radical promise—to, no matter the circumstance, always tell the truth. Each testified that their courageous pledge generated dynamism beyond anything they ever imagined, and that their relationship had grown to transcend all others.

- **Modeling and initiative:** How can we ask someone to do what we are ourselves reluctant to do? Ideally, each participant will bring initiative and leadership to the arrangement. There are times, though, when everyone slinks to the sidelines. In a tricky moment when nobody knows what to do, let this be our policy: we go first; we take the risks. While this approach guarantees moments when we will end up looking silly, it also enlivens the prospect of keeping the relationship vigorous. If we disclose some of our own deeper thoughts and feelings and present ourselves honestly, as less than fully composed, then over time our compatriots may share more of their unique truth as well.

  With many gains available only by way of trial and error, risks must be taken. A committed adoptive father observed, "We've entered into some unpredictable encounters with the birthfamilies of our children because we are convinced these connections— even if they are not entirely pleasant—are important to our kids. Actually, they are important for all of us. What's interesting is that the kids notice. Our willingness to step into uncertainty registers with them. They're at an age when they are not inclined to give us credit for very much, but this bit of stretching scores more than a few points with them."

- **Find the common ground:** It is not always easy to discover, but there is always common ground to be found. Sometimes it starts weakly—an adoptive father and birthfather who were elated to discover a shared contempt for kitchen curtains come to mind—but there are additional commonalities to be unearthed, and most of these discoveries will be more consequential. Our shared interests give us safe and rewarding territory to enjoy and build on.

- **Create common ground:** If we discover the scary truth that we have hardly anything in common, we may have to manufacture some shared experience. We can join in on each other's interests or perhaps we can develop interests or traditions that are new to all of us. One set of birth- and adoptive families, for example, settled into a pattern of watching the Super Bowl together. They are not especially rabid fans of football and they are unsure how this tradition emerged, but they all look forward to their time together watching the festivities.

- **Enjoy the uncommon ground:** Some participants are delighted to discover that they are not identical to their counterparts. Commenting on the birthparents of his child, one adoptive father mused, "Thank goodness they are so much more interesting than we are. It's a hoot to hang out with them." When viewed open-mindedly, the differences embodied in others present pleasing opportunities to expand personal horizons.

- **Acknowledge differences and clarify boundaries:** Our appraisal of others is often multilayered; we typically approve of some dimensions while we fret about others. The spirit in which we approach differences is of great importance. Again Father de Béthune offers wisdom. "Differences are important; they must be taken into account, but without exaggerating their power to divide" (2002, p. 49). We need to celebrate as much as we can, accept as much as we can, tolerate as much as we can, and then set clear, consistent, and constructive boundaries to deal with that which we deem unacceptable.

There may be some things about which we fundamentally disagree. Some of us are tempted to gloss over these touchy issues so we can maintain the illusion of like-mindedness, but these are likely the subjects we most need to clarify. We need to know where our ideas diverge and how we intend to handle these differences. If we are clear about each other's boundaries, chances are we will get along better. Homan and Pratt write insightfully about the significance of boundaries in their impressive book, *Radical Hospitality*. "The real meaning of *boundaries* is the insistence that I will not be violated by your selfishness" (2002, p. 175). Dr. Michael Kinnamon puts it this way: "Saying yes to the stranger means saying no to those things that harm the stranger" (July 1999).

Boundary setting is not an adversarial act; we set boundaries in all of our relationships and are well served by them. There is no reason to treat adoptive relationships as out of the ordinary. In their peerless guide *The Open Adoption Experience*, authors Lois Melina and Sharon Roszia suggest that one way to describe the progress we have made in adoption is to recognize that we have installed boundaries where there used to be walls.

> Walls, like the old Berlin Wall, are impenetrable. Boundaries, like border crossings, allow for decisions to be made about when they can be crossed. Walls are put up by fearful people, willing to sacrifice some possible good to be sure that all the bad will be kept out. Boundaries are put up by people who are confident of their ability to differentiate the positive from the negative and willing to take the chance that occasionally something adverse might cross the boundary in order to assure that the boundary will be accessible to all the positive things that might be available. (1993, p. 21)

In personal conversation, Roszia debunks the idea that adoptive relationships are strange and different.

> When people ask me how to handle various situations, I ask them how they handle Uncle Charley when he exhibits the same sort of questionable behavior. Adoptive relationships are no different than other family relationships; they are not as exotic as we make them out to be. (conversation with the author, January 2006)

Effective boundary management generates a milieu of safety. A sense of safety, of course, is fundamental to all relationships, and this is especially true when children are involved. The foremost duty adults hold relative to children is to keep them safe. On this there can be no compromise.

Conscientious parents work hard to create a physical and social environment for their children that is stimulating and safe. There is no way to create a hazard-free circumstance, but they do their best to reduce risks to their child's well-being by setting important limits. From time to time the rest of us may wonder about some of their policies, but we do not doubt that this is entirely their responsibility to manage and we do not begrudge them their efforts in this regard. Keeping the youngster safe is their job, and we expect them to excel in it.

- **Help each other:** Our counterparts render an important service when they coach us and give us a few pointers regarding the way things work in their world. We can do the same. I may not know much about the workings of their neighborhood, but I have a pretty good handle on mine. A bit of timely, gentle, good-natured coaching can spare all of us some embarrassing blunders.

- **Double-check for clarity:** When things seem confusing or obscure, it makes sense to slow down and make the effort to communicate with dazzling clarity. That means double-checking for meaning, and then checking one more time for good measure. Even so, no matter how hard everyone works to communicate clearly, there will be misunderstandings.

- **Seek and grant forgiveness:** Unintended slights and misunderstandings are inevitable. That means that forgiveness will need to be sought and granted in lavish doses. Forgiveness provides extra chances to get it right—opportunities everyone will need sooner or later. When difficult moments are worked through with grace, relationships are strengthened.

- **Practice reciprocity:** We will be awkward givers if we are reluctant receivers. In the best adoptive relationships, there is reciprocity, and time is cheerfully spent in both domains. An astute and poetic birthmother put it this way: "We need to walk each other's land and greet each other's dogs." Nouwen also warned about unbalanced relationships. "When only one gives and the other receives, the giver will soon become an oppressor and the receivers, victims" (1994, p. 89).

Hospitious Conversation

When birthparents and adoptive parents with little in common come together, the pressing question is, "Can we talk?" That is an essential question because the art of hospitality is in many ways the art of conversation. The stuff that goes into hospitality—goodwill, respect, courage, noticing, listening, and making room—is the same stuff that goes into constructive conversation. Conversation is a natural expression of hospitality. It is both metaphor and mechanism for openness and hospitality.

Lively conversation does not fear difference. In fact, effective conversationalists scan for difference and angle toward it, for it is in the exploration of differences where the greatest gains are made. Plowing through familiar ground is safe and sometimes pleasant, but it adds little to the pool of shared information. Discussion of differences, though, contributes greatly when conducted in a spirit of goodwill, for it is in the wrestling with differences that synergistic decision-making emerges.

Recently an expectant mother living in a homeless shelter selected the most affluent couple in our pool of available families as candidates to adopt her baby. We did our best to prepare these families for the significant lifestyle differences they would encounter, but we were concerned. We worried that they would have a difficult time achieving a sense of togetherness.

We underestimated both families—the strength of the expectant mother and the gutsy transparency of the prospective adoptive parents. While the expectant mother held little conventional social power, she was formidable as an advocate for her child. In that capacity, she was a force to reckon with. On her child's behalf, she rose up and energetically probed the souls of these folks who aspired to stand in her place. A little taken aback by the range and bluntness of her questions, yet delighted by her devotion to the baby, each of the would-be parents took a deep breath and fully entered the conversation. They had not anticipated questions about speaking in tongues and the ways fertility clinics collect specimens, but, catching the rhythm and energy of the conversation, they held nothing back and forthrightly answered every line of inquiry while raising a few pointed questions of their own. It was an amazing coming together—"exhilarating," the prospective adoptive parents would later say—and by the time the conversation wound down, their differences no longer amounted to much. They were in this thing together, energized by each other's emotional availability and by their determination to do right by the expected child. What is more, they looked to the future with confidence because, no matter what it held, they knew they could work through the issues. They could talk.

That intensely candid discussion reworked the power differential between them. Their courage enabled them to experience the hospitious transformation described by Sister Susan Smith: "To be hospitable is to change *power over* to *power with*...Vulnerability is replaced by the solidarity of belonging" (1993, pp. 41-42). Such is the potential of conversation.

Some introductory conversations are less magical. An encounter between another expectant mother and hope-filled couple comes to mind. In an effort to describe the excitement he felt at the thought of becoming a parent, the misty-eyed prospective adoptive father directed a question to the lady who was wondering whether he and his wife were the right people to parent her expected child. "Have you ever been there," he asked, voice trembling with emotion, "when a boy shoots his first bird?" During the oxygen-sapping silence that followed, hard on the heels of the expectant mother's astonished grimace, I privately thought, "Or have you ever been there when a well-meaning fellow shoots his prospects to smithereens with an ill-advised line of illustration?" To say the least, it was a lackluster conversational gambit, but they survived the gaffe and moved on to more promising subject matters.

The best conversations and relationships feature authentic listening, and the task of bridging differences requires generous amounts of it. Sincere listening is exhausting work, but it need not be grim. Vibrant conversation is often playful. Just because our child's happiness hinges on our ability to work through our differences, do we have to be so serious about all this? The differences that loom so ominous in one light can be comical in another. Laughter rounds off the edges of difference. Humor, of course, holds risks of its own. It can backfire, but it can also change the conversational tone from labored to liberating. For those with a comedic streak and the courage to unleash it, difference is a gift—the greater the differences, the richer the material they have to work with.

In hospitable adoptions, the conversation never ends. Circumstances change, and interpersonal differences expand and shrink. Through it all, constructive conversation can keep the arrangement adaptive and healthy. If the adults involved in an adoption find ways to appreciate and manage their differences, the child will benefit. If the adults grow to genuinely accept each other, she too will feel the homey satisfaction of acceptance.

CHAPTER 9

HOSPITIOUS AVAILABILITY:
Privacy as Friend and Foe

No one wants to say an ill word about hospitality. It's up there with seeing-eye dogs, designated drivers, recycling, and cancer research in the pantheon of unassailable ideas. I am confident even the crabbiest among us will concede it is a noble ideal, but I am equally certain there are detractors, and I am pretty sure I know what they want to talk about. They want to shift the discussion from hospitality to a consideration of privacy. It is a smart move. Rather than attempting to discredit an appealing concept, they counter it with another appealing concept. Their argument merits consideration. What happens when hospitality and privacy intersect?

We have described hospitality as a willingness to open our lives to others and make room for them. Since privacy can be described as a decision to keep others at a distance and not make room for them, it appears that we are about to consider a collision of two credible ideals. To some extent we are, yet we need to recognize that there is more to the interplay of hospitality and privacy than conflict. While there are times when the assertion of privacy is clearly at odds with hospitality, there are many other occasions when it enables and furthers it. In this discussion we begin by acknowledging the importance of privacy. With that significance fully recognized, we consider the ways hospitality both requires and respects privacy. Then, after asserting the importance of availability as a counterweight to excessive privacy, we conclude by considering some privacy applications that are clearly at odds with the spirit of hospitality.

The Importance of Privacy

Let's begin by stating the obvious: Some things need to be kept private. Simply put, that which is at our most intimate core is not for everyone to know. Vulnerabilities that are exploitable, raw ideas and emotions that are germinating and need time to ripen, affection made valuable by its exclusivity, mystical yearnings, and body functions are examples of personal matters that are best kept private. It is not an exaggeration to state that our sense of dignity depends on our ability to manage these intimacies to our satisfaction. If this control is lost, we feel exposed and diminished. On these matters, the importance of privacy is indisputable.

Not only does privacy protect us from unwelcome intrusion, it also serves the interests of those around us. Embarrassed, we protest "Too much information!" when someone shares too many personal details or shares them too quickly. Most of the time, we are more than happy to respect the boundaries that surround the affairs of others. These limits make sense to us. We recognize that we are easier to be around when we hold our nastiest impressions and opinions to ourselves, and we believe this is true for others as well. It makes sense to keep darker thoughts private, and many people believe that even good deeds are more meritorious if kept under hat.

Privacy and Hospitality Working Together

Although we often cast privacy as the enemy of hospitality, authentic hospitality actually requires it. As much as the spirit of hospitality promotes courageous availability and hopes to connect with others, it is careful not to intrude on them. It knows when to back off. While it invites and welcomes personal sharing, it does not press or pry. Expressions of goodwill that ignore personal boundaries are intrusive and fail as gestures of hospitality. In the art of making room, respect for the privacy of others is an essential factor.

Privacy is also essential to any sustained expression of hospitality. Without it, hospitators are at risk to burn out. Some expressions of hospitality are easily offered, but many forms are exhausting and sap our strength. Privacy gives us a chance to recover that strength. Mediator Carl Schneider writes, "In private, one can relax, blow off steam, recoup after encounters with difficult and unbearable people. This release is a safety valve; it lessens personal tension and makes social relations endurable" (1997, p. 41). Or, to borrow and adapt some words from Irish rhetoric, privacy is good for "shaking off the vexations, cares, pomps, vanities, and etiquettes of life" (Lynch, 2005, p. 107). It slows the pace and reduces the emotional load. The going seems easier when we are able to stop fretting about what others think. As we ventilate and ponder and play under the protection of privacy, we regain perspective and vitality. With our energy eventually renewed, we are ready for another round of noticing, listening, and making room.

Tension Between Privacy and Availability

We have seen that hospitality, insofar as it strives to create a context in which a person is safe to be himself and in which he is protected from demands toward conformity, is fully compatible with privacy's goal of protecting the sanctity of each person's inner being. Since hospitality aspires to interpersonal validation and connection, it parts ways when privacy is invoked to keep others at an extraordinary distance, a distance that exceeds reasonable expectations. While the amount that is disclosed and the way it is disclosed is for each person to manage, it is clear that some disclosure of personal information is necessary if there is to be any prospect for connection. Our decisions regarding disclosure are consequential. If we go too far in sharing information, we feel exposed, and we generate discomfort in those around us. If we share too little information, we run the risk of isolation. Philosopher Hannah Arendt described the toll exacted by excessive privacy:

> To live an entirely private life means above all to be
> deprived of things essential to a truly human life...The

privation of privacy lies in the absence of others; as far as they are concerned, private man does not appear, and therefore it is as though he did not exist. Whatever he does remains without significance and consequence to others, and what matters to him is without interest to other people. (1956, p. 58)

Arendt's words are piercing. By her account, extensive privacy claims an unexpected victim; it marginalizes the one who denies others access as much or more than it does the denied. Even more critically, she points to the cost of full-blown privacy. It is no trifle. In her view, privacy can be a gateway to insignificance and virtual nonexistence.

Her insights are important because they call us to think carefully about our culture's idealization of personal independence. We feel the tug of this ideal, but we do well to ponder its value. Is self-sufficiency truly desirable? Does it produce satisfaction, or does it bring loneliness? And in a globally intertwined economic reality, does it make sense for us to fancy ourselves capable of independence? Perhaps we pursue an illusion.

We are more the product of our social context than we might care to admit. It shapes our thoughts and emotions and frames our sense of value and purpose. We are intrigued by independence, but our deepest longings are for acceptance and connection. Granted, we need protection from our community's intrusion, but we also need that community to take interest in us. We violate boundaries when we intrude on the rightful privacy of others, but just as certainly we violate boundaries when we maintain distance that frustrates their reasonable expectations for connection. If ever we lose our sense of community, we flounder.

This reminder of the importance of social networks is germane because our appraisal of privacy largely depends on whether we attach primacy to the individual or to the community. Those who are attracted to the myth of personal autonomy tend to have a positive view of privacy while those who place high value on the importance of community typically view privacy less favorably. Coming from a view that accentuates community, Eugene Peterson, a gifted biblical translator, pulls no punches. "*Private* in its root meaning refers to theft. It is stealing" (1991, p. 6). From his perspective, privacy unilaterally *deprives* others of the prospect of connection which is rightly theirs. Peterson's observation suggests it is a mistake to view privacy only through the lens of individual rights; our thinking about privacy needs to consider its impact on others as well. This raises an interesting question: When adoptive participants decide to not share information with the others involved, is the information reasonably withheld, or is it pilfered?

Claims to privacy, then, are best not made lightly, for they carry the risk of isolation, and imply thievery. When potential adoptive parents assert their right to be left alone, it is possible that their wishes will be followed even more than they would like. That is to say, birthparents are not likely to choose unknowable persons as parents for their children. On those decidedly private terms, there is little prospect for adoption. Claims to privacy that might be reasonable in ordinary circumstances must yield to the necessities of disclosure if there is to be any possibility of adoption. Moreover, if we are faithful to the principle that adoption is meant to serve children, the usual claims that adoptive parents and birthparents have to privacy must defer to the adoptive child's right to know.

Adoption's days of extensive privacy, also known as secrecy, are fading fast, but we are still sorting out what merits disclosure and what is best kept private. The ratio of privacy to availability is of great significance to everyone involved and deserves lively and candid discussion as plans are negotiated. "Wrongful adoption" court cases have fortified the right of adoptive parents to fully know the background of the children they adopt, but the rights of adoptive persons and birthparents to know the facts are less established. Equity suggests there is ground to gain in this regard. The fact that adoptive persons, after decades of effort to open records, are still struggling for the right to basic information about their own history is almost incomprehensible. Of all the claims to the right to know, theirs is most compelling.

More About Availability

Availability involves three dimensions: access to pertinent information, the prospect of face-to-face interaction, and emotional acknowledgment. As helpful as it is to know about someone, it is more significant to be in contact with him, and as good as it is to interact with someone person to person, it is more meaningful to forge a mutually significant emotional connection. If I am fully available to you, you will know what you need to know about me, you will have a claim on my time and physical presence, and, because you are important to me, you will have my complete attention. Fully hospitious adoptions feature all three dimensions.

The "need to know" could hardly be higher as participants design and carry out their plans. Prospective birthparents need extensive information about potential adoptive parents in order to select the most appropriate family, and once their entrustment is complete, they need continuing reassurance that the youngster is alive and well. For their part, adoptive parents need to know a great deal about birthparents before they commit to a long-term relationship with them. They need comprehensive information, too, to effectively fill their parental roles and to provide appropriate medical care. For the child, the need to know is exceedingly high. It is, after all, *his* story, and he requires first-rate information to make sense of it all. It is the responsibility of the adults involved to make sure each child is lovingly told the full story.

The "need for connection" is also high. It is one thing for prospective birthparents to know *about* prospective adoptive parents, but it is far more significant to meet them and get to know them. Prospective birthparents need to come into their presence, look them in the eye, and weigh their souls before there's any chance of entrusting a child to them. Birthparents need access to the family, too, so they can express their continuing affection directly to the youngster. Testimonials to the love of birthparents are meaningful, but these assurances are more convincing when they are delivered personally and backed up with affectionate behavior. Adoptive children delight in first-hand, tangible evidence that all of the people who are important to them love them. Unlike the one-dimensional nature of information conveyed through words alone, face-to-face interaction is richly textured. Everyone has a better grasp of the overall gestalt when they interact directly.

As important as information and direct personal connection are, the "need to matter" is even more significant. An adoption featuring substantial information and contact but lacking emotional availability leaves many of the child's most basic needs unmet. Emotional availability is openness in its highest form; it is the goal child-centered adoption proponents seek. Adoptions that surround children with emotionally available adults hold the most potential to recognize and meet their needs. Adoptive families in which noticing, listening, and making room are practiced arts do not necessarily have it easy, but emergent issues are accessible in these families, and that means they are positioned to address questions and devise new patterns of interaction. Children who grow up in safe, interested, nonjudgmental, nurturing, and supportive environments—truly open families—are free to explore, at a pace of their own choosing, the issues of greatest interest to them. If the adults they are counting on are less available or emotionally remote, these explorations carry greater psychic risk.

Misapplications of Privacy

Let me reiterate an earlier point. No one disputes the need that everyone involved in adoption has for privacy. We cannot sustain close connection to others without it. But here is my worry: I believe there are times when otherwise thoughtful people invoke privacy not for the sake of protecting matters that are intimate, but for the sake of personal ease and convenience. Once their most pressing needs are met, they lose interest in cooperation. Suddenly, the experience is all about them; they are no longer their brother's keeper. They may cloak their pursuit of the convenient path with the righteous language of privacy, but their claims are not persuasive. They are not protecting sacred intimacy; they are hiding from it, and their course of action is decidedly inhospitable.

Another version of privation occurs when parents practice a form of love that is exclusive and possessive. Smitten by a fascinating child whom they now claim as their own, they conclude that he is too wonderful to be shared and disavow their prior declarations of welcome. In this insecure frame of mind, no one is allowed to draw close to the youngster. They are especially chilly in response to those whom they fear might compete for his affection. As fear swells and carries the day, community shrinks. No longer willing to make room for others, they signal the birthfamily that it would be best if they moved on. Again, the cover for this ethical downshift is privacy.

Can these willful assertions of privacy for the sake of convenience or possession succeed? Severson offers insight on this. Questioned whether he thinks adoptive parents ought to be able to protect their privacy, he responds,

> Yes I do. I want them to be able to lock their front door. I want them to be able to put a 'No Trespassing' sign in their front yard. But I don't think it makes much difference if your house is haunted. And that's what closed adoption does. It fills your house with ghosts, with attics and closets that can't be opened, with questions that can't be answered, with questions that can't be asked. (1991, p. 107)

Privacy may succeed at keeping others at bay, but it is more likely to fuel curiosity than to quell it.

Benefiting from Balance

Privacy and hospitality are not inherently at odds. In fact, most of the time they work in tandem, and the families of adoption benefit from each. It is only when privacy is asserted in a manner that restricts reasonable availability that it runs counter to the spirit of hospitality. When privacy is invoked for the sake of convenience or possession, it deprives others of the information and access they deserve. In that vein, privacy inhospitably destroys community. In that vein, privacy renders a child's world artificially small.

Just as privacy functions best within limits, so does hospitality. Even the most gregarious among us must occasionally restrict availability to others because it is impossible to maintain close connections with everyone who comes along. Since our various relationships are not of equal importance, our availability to others naturally corresponds to the importance we attach to the relationship. One of the assumptions of child-centered adoption is that all the participants are in the experience together. Fates are forever linked, and the delight or distress of one will affect the others. Given that reality, it makes sense to place a high priority on these relationships, and, in the spirit of hospitality, it makes sense for adoptive parents, birthparents, and adoptive persons to commit themselves to high levels of availability.

Availability is healthiest when kept in creative tension with privacy. Adoptive parents need to be available to their journeymates, but they also need to be free to carry out their parental responsibilities unencumbered. They are not babysitters; they are parents, and the difference is enormous. Likewise, birthparents have a right to contain and control the most intimate details of their story. More importantly, adoptive parents and birthparents need to collectively protect their child's story. They need to divulge details judiciously so their sons and daughters have time to grow into its intricacies. Since there are many contributors to every adoption story, there are potentially many tellers of the tale. One hopes information is shared with discretion, for in the end the story belongs to the child. It is his to grow into.

The interplay of privacy and availability never ends. In some instances privacy will make the stronger claim and in others availability will carry the day. The determination requires fair-minded deliberation that takes the child's need for availability into account. One hopes his needs will trump all claims of privacy invoked by birthfamilies and adoptive families for the sake of comfort or convenience.

CHAPTER 10

WELCOMING THE WELCOMERS:
How Agencies Make Room for Programs Based on Hospitality

Those who work in the field of adoption with the goal of being fully available to people in need are themselves in need of a welcoming and supportive system. They will have a difficult time making others feel at home unless they are securely at home in their own organization. This organizational hospitality cannot be presumed; it is anything but automatic. Rather, institutional support for the hospitable practice of adoption is a gift, a bold expression of an agency's faith in an ancient ideal and its modern-day proponents. Like all forms of hospitality, this systemic welcome requires substantial goodwill, respect, and courage.

Although most nonprofit organizations are rooted in the tradition of hospitality, it is difficult for an organization to "make room" for an adoption program that is committed to the ideals of hospitality. Since almost all of the reality factors pressuring contemporary nonprofit agencies run counter to the ideals of hospitality, programs of this ilk are very difficult to host and manage. Child welfare agencies are rightly concerned about efficiency and accountability. In the handling of scarce charitable resources, these modern organizational values are of great importance. After all, dollars need stretching and funding sources need reassuring. The trouble with these sensible mandates is that they just don't jibe with the spirit of hospitality.

Theologian Pohl describes the tension well. She writes,

> Much of the provision of help today is given by social serv-
> ice professionals in a context of careful management,
> effective technique, clearly defined roles, and complex
> regulations. Hospitality, on the other hand, is a "form of
> relationship that is essentially unspecialized." The rela-
> tionships fostered within the practice of hospitality
> implicitly challenge bureaucratic rules that reinforce sep-
> aration, isolation, and anonymity. Hospitality suggests
> ways to break down the barriers between provider and
> client that are essential to the entire "service" orientation.
> Hospitality offers a model for developing more reciprocal
> relationships. (1991, p. 162)

She further explains, "A distinctive feature of many contemporary advocates of hospitality rather than 'service' is their rejection
of bureaucratic styles of helping. They stress minimal scrutiny and
focus instead on respect and friendship" (p. 163). As Pohl's observations make clear, hospitality operates in a way that chafes against
the strictures of today's social agency.

Is it possible to reconcile this tension between the demands of
modern organizations and bull-headed practitioners of hospitality?
Can an administrator justify support for an anachronistic (or is it
cutting edge?) program based on the ideals of hospitality? If this is a
practice style she can endorse, how does she manage it? How does
she shepherd it into the fold of acceptable modern practice? These
are questions that require answers if hospitable programs are to
persevere. Already ruffling the system through their advocacy for
low status clients, child-centered adoption workers will find it difficult if not impossible to practice hospitality if their agencies
systemically discourage it.

When, as they are wont to do, a board of directors decides it is
time to bring in an efficiency consultant to pare away the organization's "fat," a program based on hospitality is in for a challenging
time. A convincing case will need to be made for a very thoughtful
application of efficiency principles, or the hospitable nature of the

program will be at risk. It is in jeopardy because the values of efficiency and hospitality do not easily coexist. As they "tweak the system" and "tighten things down a bit," efficiency experts are on the lookout for wasted effort or moments when it seems little of note is happening to propel the process forward. Unfortunately, the stuff they squeeze out of a program—the activities that are nondescript and difficult to quantify—is its hospitality. Although adoption workers know that low-agenda time spent mixing with participants often pays the highest dividends, this use of scarce resources strikes consultants as dubious.

Hospitality-minded adoption workers have three concerns about efficiency. First, they see it as largely irrelevant to their work. In their view, efficiency sheds little light on ways to enhance or deepen their connection to clients. Second, they worry that an emphasis on efficiency can distort the way adoption is conceptualized and practiced. Third, they believe there are times when efficiency is undesirable. That is to say, they contend that a naturally inefficient course will often produce better results than an artificially efficient one. Given these concerns, and with an eye toward irony, they view efficiency studies as a waste of time.

Our faster-is-better culture is enamored with efficiency. Accustomed to ever-swifter results, we are impatient with deliberative or circuitous processes. We think a dose of efficiency will make every circumstance better, but hospitality-sensitive thinkers know there are some endeavors where it lacks relevance. Does it make sense, for example, to apply the ideal of efficiency to art, worship, or the expression of emotion? Shall we find satisfaction in a hymn sung efficiently? Does it make sense to think about grieving efficiently? Is efficiency a variable of interest as we develop our friendships? When it comes to matters of heart and spirit—adoption comes to mind— efficiency has little to offer.

An even larger concern for hospitality proponents is that efficiency can distort our understanding of adoption and our practice of it. Two things are likely to happen when we approach adoption with a bent toward efficiency: It alters our sense of the time frame involved, and it discounts the psychological complexity of the experience. Instead of conceptualizing adoption as a lifelong journey, it is reduced to a placement process. And instead of embracing the emotional richness of adoption, it is treated as merely a mechanical process. Through the lens of efficiency, there is nothing special about the work of adoption. It is simply one more human service offering on a long list of possibilities.

Hospitious practitioners are obliged to protest this austere view of adoption; it is an apprehension that is seriously misaligned with our everyday experience. Our firsthand encounters with adoption generate a very different understanding of what is being asked of us. We know that adoption roils with drama and emotion, and we know as we continually field calls from searching birthparents and adoptive persons that the activities leading to placement are not the entirety of the experience. Better understood, adoption is a lively, intriguing, enduring, and continually evolving set of relationships. Adoption records are held permanently for a reason; the experience lasts a lifetime. When we take the long view of adoption and see it as a lifelong experience, time and effort spent on hospitality suddenly looks more efficient than they did in the short term, because chances are good that adoptions founded on hospitality will require fewer community resources through the years than those that result from a streamlined process.

Additionally, an emphasis on efficiency distorts our understanding of adoption in another significant way. By elevating the measurable aspects of adoption at the expense of its intangibles, this emphasis understates the existential dimensions involved. The emphasis on procedure reduces adoption to a mechanical transaction bordering on the impersonal. Accomplishing tasks becomes more important than responding to people. For some, suspicious of esoteric depictions of adoption, that hard-nosed rendering of the subject is just right. They believe adoption is little more than an exchange to be worked out, and they are annoyed with talk of its spiritual implications. For those who are convinced that adoption carries many dimensions of meaning, however, this impoverished approach seriously misses the mark. Procedures are important, but they are in service to a greater reality—the coming together of families by way of a sacred covenant—and they are ineffective if they are not imbued with respectful attitudes. Hospitality advocates know that much of the really important work of adoption is indirect. What others might consider peripheral is, in their view, indispensable. Sometimes all we can do for each other is to be there to ponder the uncertainties side by side. Not much goes on when one is just there, but that simple presence contains the power to radically transform relationships.

Hospitality proponents believe there are times when the inefficient course is the most desirable path to follow. When the bends and crooks of a river are straightened to facilitate navigation, something is gained, but something is also lost. Traffic on the river moves more efficiently, but the river's capacity to handle floodwaters is diminished. Perhaps the bends and turns of adoption are similarly inconvenient, and similarly functional. The meanderings of adoption offer occasions to test and strengthen relationships. They decelerate the process, providing participants more time and experience to ponder their responsibilities and deepen their connections. The fits and starts that characterize emerging adoptive relationships add humor and history to the shared story. This naturalized process is important because the coming together of prospective adoptive parents and prospective birthparents can feel strained or contrived, especially in the early stages when it carries the feel of urgency. Birthparents and adoptive parents need time to normalize their relationship and grow into their commitments. In Severson's words, "When it comes to adoption, it is never well for it to be done quickly" (1991, p. 78). Relationships need time to ripen; they have less flavor and substance when they are hurried. Adoptions are built on trust. They only move forward when trust runs high, and the building of trust takes time.

The tension between contemporary management strategies and hospitality is striking. Each perspective has value, and one might suppose the debate between them is vigorous and protracted. This is hardly the case. When these different ways of going about adoption compete for support from an organization's management team, the voice of efficiency almost always prevails. The hospitable view persists and has standing only through the grace and courage of the hospitious administrator. Against the currents of the day that cast the practice of adoption as a business endeavor, she preserves the ideal that this work is a service to children motivated by a sense of mission. She is certainly not oblivious to organizational issues of productivity. It matters to her, but she places higher priority on making sure the work expresses the organization's value system. She shares every administrator's determination to keep the budget balanced, but the real joy of her work is in seeing the program's constituency treated with dignity and grace.

The hospitable administrator knows the essential issue is effectiveness, not efficiency. For proponents of hospitality, this is an important distinction. When effectiveness is the goal, efficiency is not automatically presumed to be a great good; it is useful only to the extent it contributes to improved outcomes. There are times when streamlined procedures may lead to better results, but there are other times when they may not. A virtue of the effectiveness perspective and its interest in qualitative outcomes is that it prompts us to become very clear regarding program goals. Are we interested in making placements—a short-term event—or do we intend to create adoptions that are likely to blossom into enduring, child-serving relationships? The way we answer that question will likely determine whether we opt for efficiency or hospitality.

The hospitality-minded administrator, then, speaks the language of effectiveness. She understands ideas and challenges in terms of what they mean for the clientele, not as requirements that satisfy the system's need for productivity. And instead of talking about efficiency, she speaks about the stewardship of scarce resources. Her hospitality takes the form of a continuous conversation with the staff as to what is being accomplished. Her willingness to listen assures them that their efforts to welcome and make room for others are noticed and respected. From listening she realizes that some situations come together relatively simply while others hold many complications.

That knowledge leads her to resist the pressures toward standardizing the process into a one-size-fits-all mold. The greatest service an effective administrator renders to her staff is to manage the budget in a way that liberates workers from excessive concern about financial matters.

The pressures impinging on hospitality are the very factors that make it so attractive and necessary. The more people entering the adoption arena, operating in an economic milieu that wants to use them and squeeze more out of them, the more refreshing hospitality looms. The productivity trends that threaten the practice of hospitality also multiply its appeal. If the threat is weathered, opportunity awaits. The spirit of hospitality satisfies the deep desire participants have for connection and camaraderie. One hopes administrators recognize this deep longing and respond to their constituencies hospitably, but, as was noted at the outset, this recognition cannot be presumed. In today's world, the easier and safer path for the CEO is to go along with prevailing managerial strategies. For hospitality to move forward as a viable model for the practice of adoption, administrators will need to manage their programs with extraordinary conviction and courage.

CHAPTER 11

CHILD-CENTERED HOSPITALITY:
The Next Phase of Openness

Now that the campaigns for and against open adoption have calmed and openness has achieved a measure of general acceptance, it is time to pin down the meaning of the word. For decades we wrangled about the wisdom of doing adoption openly, but these disputes were never conducted with well-defined terms. Even among proponents of openness, there was little consensus as to its meaning. Talking about open adoption is akin to talking about democracy. We may think we are discussing something obvious, but there are many variations on the theme, and the variations matter enormously. Since confusion gives rise to misunderstanding and misunderstanding too often leads to profound disappointment, it is worth the effort to work towards greater clarity of meaning.

With its multiple elements, open adoption is almost impossible to succinctly define. Efforts to condense it into simple form invariably leave out very important dimensions. Comprehensively understood, open adoption is a rope of many important strands.

- **Information:** A hallmark of open adoption is that everyone involved is well informed. The parties are not hidden from each other; they are identified and fully known. The information they share is direct and comprehensive, with updates as needed.

- **Communication:** Participants interact in many forms. Face-to-face contact is the most important form of interaction, but families stay in touch by mail, phone, and e-mail as well. The frequency of communication varies widely.

- **Attitudes:** The way birthparents, adoptive parents, and adoptive persons view each other is paramount because their attitudes color all their interactions. If their attitudes are constructive, chances are strong that their interactions will be as well. Running through the highest forms of open adoption are the attitudes of respect, courage, and goodwill.

- **Relationships:** Relationships are at the heart of open adoption. Minimally, open adoptions feature relationships between adoptive parents, birthparents, and adoptive children. In robustly open adoptions, entire clans mingle in interesting and meaningful ways. Prominent in these expansive relationship networks are siblings and grandparents.

- **Values:** The bedrock of open adoption is its value base. Among the most important of these values are child-centeredness, family preservation, candor, and a willingness to acknowledge the painful dimensions of the experience. Informing and flavoring the innumerable decisions made through the decades, these values hold great significance.

- **Vision:** No two open adoptions are alike; each family system is uniquely shaped by its members. That said, it is also true that proponents of openness have a vision in mind as they help to organize these arrangements. They are pointing toward some ideal outcomes; three stand out. They hope that these adoptions will be characterized by hospitality, that the openness will take root and blossom into emotionally available families, and that over time the child will take an active role in shaping the experience.

- **Commitment:** Open adoptions are meant for the long haul. As rewarding as these relationships can be, substantial effort is required to sustain them. The work will not get done unless those involved are fully committed to the project. The idea of a half-hearted open adoption is an oxymoron.

- **Adaptation:** One of the great benefits of openness is that it enables families to adjust course according to emerging and accumulating information. Families manage their adoptions more effectively as they learn from experience.

- **Spirituality:** When an adoption comes together with authentic openness, everyone involved is left a little dumbfounded. Far more transpires than anyone can begin to explain. A rich and peculiar conglomeration of sacrifice, courage, truth, and compassion, hospitious openness contains intimations of the divine.

The multi-dimensionality of open adoption makes it difficult to discuss. Must an adoption feature every strand to be considered open? Probably not. Is an adoption open if it involves only one dimension of openness? Again, probably not. Because open adoption involves so many factors, subjectivity is inescapable. Rather than frustrate ourselves trying to make either/or distinctions, we may get further ahead by addressing the extent of an adoption's openness. Whenever we encounter openness claims, the prudent response is to assume very little and to ask which elements of openness the adoption features. "Help me understand. In what ways is your adoption open?"

We are approaching a point where virtually every adoption incorporates some dimensions of openness. In the words of University of Texas researcher Dr. Ruth McCroy, "Confidentiality is no longer the norm" ("New Adoption Study," 2002). Restating that observation affirmatively, it is evident that openness is now the norm in the adoption of infants. Openness is the new default. Whereas it was formerly presumed that an adoption would be closed unless a case could be made for opening it, we now presume it will be open unless there are persuasive reasons for restriction. As the awareness takes hold that in most cases a reference to adoption presupposes openness factors, the adjective *open* becomes redundant, and it will gradually drop out of use to describe adoption.

As *open* fades as a useful qualifier, we are left with a void. Clearly, adoptions are far from uniform in the forms they take. Some are chilly and contentious while others exude warmth and solidarity. How do we account for the differences between them? The answer may very well be found in the realm of hospitality. In the contemporary practice of adoption, we can presume fairly extensive information sharing, but we cannot presume hospitality. Some adoptions manifest a spirit of inclusion; some don't. Some acknowledge and welcome an array of players while others energetically narrow the field. Some brim with goodwill while others radiate distrust. As we appraise and describe the adoptions of the future, hospitality will be a key differentiating factor.

When adoptions lack hospitality, there is not much life to them. The fact of adoption sits at the family doorstep as an awkward fact of life, but little is done to address its implications. Hospitious adoptions are another story. When participants aspire to more than exchanging information, when they commit to being fully available to each other, possibilities abound. Picnics grow larger. Aging relatives stay in touch. Misunderstandings are worked through. Birthday presents multiply. With hospitality in the mix, interactions take on a vibrant yet relaxed tone. These ventures often generate feelings of liberation, a mixture of relief and pride and tenderness that comes from good faith efforts and from finding ways to overcome assorted barriers. When tearful garden chats are weathered and pool parties are salvaged, satisfaction takes root. There is simply more to these adoptions—more information, more support, more idealism, more fun, more challenge, more ownership, more creativity, and more grace.

Most importantly, hospitious adoptions are more child-centered. Intentional in its goal of helping children feel at home in their new circumstances, this approach is conscious of their well-being from start to finish. Adoption becomes hospitious to children when it notices, listens, and makes room for them. These are not exotic activities. Noticing happens when attentive adults are fully present to the child and are sensitive to adoption-related undercurrents. Listening happens when the atmosphere is safe and accepting and when adults are patiently available. Central to each of these skills is availability and attentiveness.

As the most complex step in hospitality, making room can be more challenging, but there are many ways to afford adoptive children the space they need. The first task is to guard against possessiveness. As wonderful as it is to heartily claim our children and exalt in their wonder, there is hazard in going too far with this energy. If it becomes possessive, it soon shrinks the child's world by driving others away. We make room for children by surrounding them with sensible boundaries. These protective limits establish a secure base from which a child can engage his surroundings. We create space for children when we advocate for them when they are too young or too fearful to voice their thoughts. Additional room is gained when we bless their interest in and interaction with their birthfamilies. These encounters depend on birthfamilies making themselves available to their children even though it may not always be convenient or emotionally comfortable. This asks a lot of them since they likely chose adoption because of heavy demands and limited resources. Nevertheless, hospitality is bold about this: The needs of the children trump the comforts of the adults. We make room for children when we let them draw their own conclusions, even when these are painful or not what we hoped to hear. Most crucially, we honor children when we respect their idiosyncrasies and accept them for who they are.

Openness set the stage for this movement toward greater child-centeredness. From its earliest days, open adoption advocates aspired to delivering a system that met the needs of children. Having listened to countless adoptive persons who grew up frustrated by the strictures of secrecy, we knew that dramatic changes in our policies and practices were required. We saw that the participants of adoption are interrelated; if any of them suffered, there were important implications for the others. We recognized the importance of attitudes, values, and relationships. The hospitality paradigm builds on these dimensions of openness and lends focus to them. It brings new energy to a cause that has made many contributions.

In particular, the open adoption movement has made great gains in its battle with secrecy, but now new challenges have arisen. It is not enough to improve the flow of information; there is much more to be done. Our foundations are shaking. The goal of putting children first is in jeopardy. We need to vigorously pound this stake back into the ground—adoption must first and foremost be a service to children. That means fending off pressures to act as if adoption is just another business endeavor whose goal is to satisfy the needs of adults. It also means working with a broader understanding of openness and shifting our emphasis from disclosure to availability. This evolution is exciting because it goes to the heart of adoption. Done well, adoption centers on the goal of helping children feel accepted and wondrously at home. Done well, adoption overflows with hospitality. Given this knowledge, we cannot stand idly by. It is time for us to speak and act as champions of hospitality.

CHAPTER 12

SPEAKING PERSONALLY:
Hospitality as an Expression of Faith

"That must be nice." Familiar words, these, to any adoption worker who has attended a school reunion. It's what classmates say when they learn there is an adoption worker in their midst, and every time I hear their comment I am jarred by the word *nice*. In their view, the work of adoption is a benign and cheerful endeavor. Well, I'll concede there surely are some pleasant aspects to the work—I have the chance to interact with folks who are working for all their worth to find a path of courage and compassion and I get out of the office quite a bit—but this word *nice* just does not work for me. The word that comes to my mind is *scary*.

I cannot imagine that anyone will ever explain the lump in the throat that comes with adoption work better than Severson.

> Because adoption does raise perennial, timeless philosophical and spiritual questions, because adoption involves matters of what Tillich called, "ultimate concern," to practice adoption requires an ongoing *auseinandersetzung* or confrontation with one's own most secret innermost spiritual self. To practice adoption ethically requires that we look through the glass darkly and confront the abyss of ourselves. And, as Nietzsche said, "He who looks too long in the abyss finds the abyss is looking back at him." Adoption work itself, then, becomes a spiritual journey, a means of polishing the heart. (1994, p. 209)

No doubt we get into the work of adoption for many reasons—some drifting into it accidentally, others thinking it might be interesting—but we linger because we find it personally meaningful. We stick with it because the work is spiritually unnerving, provocative, and illuminating. Indeed, we persevere because it gives us a chance to polish our hearts.

Perhaps it seems strange to speak of the value this work has for practitioners. I mean, isn't it supposed to be about meeting the needs of those who are going through this experience? Absolutely. What I like about Severson's insight, though, is that he makes clear that we who oversee adoption's undulating shifts of hosting and guesting are profoundly affected by our involvement in the drama and that we are ourselves works in progress. We are in the adventure, not above it. Like those we would serve, we have a lot to share and a lot to learn. If we are not spiritually engaged as practitioners, no one is well served.

Obedience

For sure, this adoption worker's heart requires plenty of polishing. I confess that I have been something of a maverick in my work. Amiable most of the time, but also stubborn, I am amused as it occurs to me that one of the reasons I am drawn to hospitality is, of all things, obedience. You see, my conviction that hospitality is the best way to approach this work is in many ways offset by my awareness of the amount of effort it requires. I could not be more convinced of its virtue, yet I find myself inventing what are, to my mind, utterly compelling excuses to avoid situations calling for hospitality. The factor that breaks my gridlock and pulls me into getting serious about hospitality is my understanding of what my faith requires of me. For people of faith, hospitality is not optional; it is obligatory. As Homan and Pratt put it, "You can't ignore people when God is looking out their eyes at you" (2002, p. 10). Or, in the words of Archbishop Tutu,

> Our God is a God who has a bias for the weak, and we
> who worship this God, who have to reflect the character
> of this God, have no option but to have a like special

concern for those who are pushed to the edges of society, for those who because they are different seem to be without a voice. (2004, p. 66)

The hospitality mandate is inescapable. Alas, when Homan and Pratt declare, "Jesus' proclamation of the kingdom of God demands a radical decision in favor of our neighbor," they leave me no wiggle room (2002, p. 45).

So, like it or not, down the hospitality trail I must go. It is my duty. I remain a gifted excuse-maker, but I go in faith, the sort of faith preacher Barbara Brown Taylor describes in *The Luminous Web*. "This is the definition of faith I want to go forward with: a radical openness to the truth, whatever it may turn out to be" (2000, p. 86). Though I relentlessly circle and backtrack, I have no choice but to set out on the path of discovery.

Counter-Culturalism

Yet another confession is in order: The maverick in me is tickled by the counter-cultural nature of hospitality. To my way of thinking, there is something sweetly pigheaded about it. People holding a more positive view of contemporary culture may not agree, but I think the ideals of hospitality run counter to prevailing values. While the mainstream is agog with tactics and strategies generating greater efficiency and productivity, hospitality plods along with little interest in achievement for achievement's sake. It counters the hurricane winds of every-man-for-himself thinking with the candle of hope that wonders if we might be of help to each other.

Our culture teaches us to crave self-sufficiency, but the goal of independence seems misguided to hospitality proponents. For their taste, an emphasis on self-sufficiency generates loneliness and leaves too many people behind. As Lucien Richard puts it, "To welcome the stranger today is to challenge the social arrangements that exclude and include; it is to challenge the conception of the self as primarily individual" (2000, p. 74). He continues, "Hospitality performs a transformation of the way one thinks. Hospitality questions one's ways of thinking about oneself and the other as belonging to different spheres; it breaks down categories that isolate" (p. 12). By challenging the we/they thinking so prevalent in everyday interaction, hospitality shakes up the status quo. In this righteous mischief, my contrary spirit takes delight.

Grace

As much as I like the genial contrariness of adoption done hospitably—the way it quietly chips away at the social order—I like even more that it is grounded in goodness and grace. Oden writes beautifully about the connection between grace and hospitality.

> For me, the central insight is that hospitality is a means of grace. It is an avenue, path, or opening to God's grace in the world in which we both receive and pass it on to others…Hospitality is a way of life infused with grace, a participation in the grace of God all around us, not a set of particular actions or behaviors. Hospitality is more a matter of becoming attuned to grace and participating in its movement than it is trying to create a particular atmosphere or situation…It may be that the best way to cultivate hospitality is to cultivate a deep awareness of God's grace and the means that open it. Only out of that awareness and gratitude can hospitality be genuinely practiced. (2001, p. 298)

I am convinced that adoptions characterized by hospitality are "attuned" to God's grace. How else do we account for the warm, transformative power of these relationships? Regularly I am the beneficiary of this grace; occasionally I am that grace to others.

York takes the idea of grace a little further. She observes,

> Some people might say of those they serve at the soup kitchen, "There but for the grace of God go I." I think what they really mean is, "There *by* the grace of God *am* I," for surely God's grace does not single some of us out for privilege and allow others to suffer. Divine grace,

however, brings us into dialogue with the stranger at the
table and the stranger within; it acquaints us with the part
of ourselves that is reflected in someone who is, by definition anyway, deemed less fortunate. (2002, p. 105)

When we muster a little hospitality and close the gap between
stranger and self, we are sure to grow. As York continues, "The best
kind of hospitality seeps into your soul and shapes your identity"
(2002, p. 114).

The next time someone comments on the "nice" and "happy"
work of adoption, I might just concede that there is an element of
truth to her assertion. I might respond saying, "You're right.
Sometimes, when I watch families interact with goodwill and
respect, I feel the warmth of hospitality seeping into my soul."

Redemption

In a perfect world we would not need adoption, but the stories of
poverty, misguided allegiance, and lousy luck routinely told in my
office remind me that we are far from done with it. The stark and
inescapable truth is that the story of adoption always begins with
brokenness and loss. Always. What is there in the repertoire of
tragedy to match the rupture of the bond between mother and child?
Who has words to describe the sickening month-by-month anguish
of infertility? Small wonder the word *primal* is important in the lex-
icon of adoption.

This brokenness is a major issue in the field of adoption. Old
schoolmates notwithstanding, it is a not-so-nice aspect of adoption,
and we are unusually creative in our ways of minimizing it. Wanting
so much for adoption to shine, we gloss over the loss that is at its
core. We ignore, deny, reframe, problem solve, and sometimes even
glorify its suffering. We do just about everything but acknowledge it
for the painful thing it is. Following a therapeutic instinct to "go to
the pain," a few tarry and do their best to contend with the losses,
but even they struggle to face the withering sadness.

Linking pain to joy, ethicist Lewis Smedes wrote, "If our joy is honest joy, it must somehow be congruent with human tragedy...Only the heart that hurts has a right to joy" (1982, p. 15). This linkage is foundational, and I believe it sets the emotional perimeters for the experience of adoption. The authenticity of our joy cannot exceed the genuineness with which we address the underlying sadness. The chipper, ain't-it-swell version of adoption that ignores its sadness is unconvincing. Its joy is hollow.

To the extent the pain is honored, the prospect of redemption emerges. It is not that adoption done well erases or nullifies the sadness. What was lost remains lost, but loss need not be the entirety of the story. When separation and disconnection are addressed with hospitality, adoption holds new potential. As we've come to realize, amazing things can happen when adoptive parents and birthparents and adoptive persons honor and make room for each other. For all its sadness, loving adoption often brims with welcome and laughter and life. In a mysterious dance that is larger than any of the individual participants, something remarkable—strangely full of pain and hope, effort and honesty—comes to stand in place of despair.

Recently I attended a worship service in a community that had long resisted any sort of openness in adoption. Not so many years ago, those who brought life to the planet without the benefit of marriage faced censure in this setting. On this day, though, the atmosphere was anything but judgmental. There was baptizing to be done, and there was celebration, too, of the fact that families had been joined and extended through adoption. With commemorative candles blazing, the baby's birthparents basked in acknowledgment and honor and support. The redemptive power of hospitality was warmly evident that morning. Because some goodhearted folks had made room for each other, shame had given way to, of all things, blessing.

Blessing

Truly, this work polishes us. It is easy to emphasize the amount of effort involved, but the practice of hospitality brims with rewards.

I like the way theologian Thomas Reynolds gets at this truth. He writes,

> In opening myself to receive another I receive something precious, not something obliged or intended as an exchange value but instead as an unintended moral consequence...It involves self-transcendence, a liberating release from the deadness of fear-based individual isolation into a life-giving mutuality of vulnerability and empowerment. The result leads us to become larger and more fully alive. I am expanded and transformed, brought into a relationship that makes me more than I was before. (2008, p. 122)

I wrote that the work of adoption feels scary, and I meant it. This work is so consequential; we bear the hopes and fears of so many. As we grow in competence and discover more and more indications of adoption's reach, we grow in awareness of how much that is vitally important we leave unattended. It is staggering to know that our fumbles as well as our acts of kindness will reverberate through communities and generations. And, if that momentousness were not enough, our work is also astonishingly intimate. We are there when destiny shows its hand, and the inner stuff of all the players is exposed. We are there when hope dies and when it shows signs of reviving, not always in that order. We are there when people want answers and there are none.

The consequential intimacy of this work is both terrible and wonderful. The magnitude of responsibility is frightening, but it also opens the prospect for profound blessings. In *Deeply Woven Roots*, Gary Gunderson writes, "This is how blessing comes to us if it comes to us at all: from one human to another in the name of all that lasts, in song, prayer, silence, word, touch, presence" (1997, p. 94). We who inhabit the world of adoption have the capacity to bless each other with simple decency. All it takes is a bit of hospitality.

CHAPTER 13

QUESTIONS AND ANSWERS:
Hospitious Implications and Applications

This last chapter is adapted from a series of conversations between the author and Daniel Wolf, a friend. In this question-and-answer format, the concepts of hospitality are applied to adoption in very practical ways.

Dan and his wife Julie are parents to two grown adoptive children. Intrigued by the complicated wonder of adoption, as he puts it, "from the first few sentences in the orientation meeting," they have been longstanding proponents of openness. Curious by nature and an international business consultant by trade, Dan has thought more about the workings of adoption than most. He is the author of 2007's *Prepared and Resolved: The Strategic Agenda for Growth, Performance and Change.*

Daniel Wolf: *What did you have in mind as you set out to write this book?*

James Gritter: We speak about adoption as if we know what we're talking about when we use the term, but the thing that stands out for me after more than 30 years in the field is how unique each adoption is. Some are astonishingly cold-hearted and others are so brave and tender and considerate they leave me gasping. I'd like this book to nudge things in that more considerate direction. Key to that goal is helping folks come to terms with the desperation that so often drives the experience. More often than not they enter this high-stakes emotional experience with their backs to the wall. No surprise, then, that so many proceed with what I'll euphemistically call "focused self-interest." I've always thought that it was my job to counter the reflex toward selfishness, and the best way I know to mitigate that impulse is to invoke the prospect of hospitality. Hospitality is a genial way to invite participants to honor and include their cohorts in the process. It's a way to keep a measure of grace in the mix.

I'm concerned that the considerable drama surrounding each placement makes short-term thinkers out of everyone involved, including me. There are so many issues pressing in on us early on that we end up more interested in just getting adoptions done than we are in helping folks get organized for the long haul. If we are going to rise above this temptation to elevate procedure over relationship building, we need compelling language and framework. So that's what I've tried to do. I've tried to describe a congenial approach to adoption that closes the gap between our rhetoric about serving children first and our practices that so often cater to the interests of the adults. I've tried to describe a way of approaching adoption that keeps us mindful of each other.

Along those lines, I'd be thrilled if this book helped us think about adoption more in terms of connection than separation. I'm not talking about glossing over the losses; those come with the territory and we need to be keenly aware of them. I am convinced, though, that if we grow to think of adoption as a means of connecting families rather than as a mechanism to replace one family with another, we brighten the story and preserve options for the youngster. Surely we need to rethink the way we depict those early, tormented decisions made by birthfamilies. Too often we treat their decision to entrust another family with the privileges and responsibilities of parenting as an act of disownership rather than as an act of loving expansion. Hospitality can change the tenor of it all from rejection and rescue to good-natured cooperation.

As I see it, the big idea in this book—the idea that can make an important difference moving forward—is that hospitality empowers the kids. It does this by viewing them as emerging hosts. If we keep the end in mind from the beginning and recognize that they are on their way toward assuming the role of ultimate host, we are far more likely to deal them in as full-fledged participants. That excites me because prior paradigms have kept them remarkably passive. Now, instead of just being along for the ride, they can at least ride shotgun. We've struggled for a long time to find ways to make adoption more child-centered, and I think the hospitality-based approach brings life to the concept. If it truly empowers the children, it will pose an appealing alternative to the commercial model of adoption that demeans them.

DW: *Any other hopes for the book?*

JG: I'd like to think that framing the practice of infant adoption in hospitable terms moves it closer to the way we work with older kids. That is to say, less effort to mimic biology and, in the language of David Kirk's classic, *Shared Fate*, more "acceptance of difference." Through the years there's been a lot of effort in the field of infant adoption to engineer similarity between birth- and adoptive families. That remains a worthwhile goal, but I've come to realize we will always fall short. I think there is a better return on our effort when we help participants find ways to acknowledge their differences and constructively tackle them. It's in helping participants handle their differences that the professionals involved can make their most crucial contributions.

DW: *What was it that set the book into motion?*

JG: It really did start with Philip Peters' remark about "the old dog ...with no place to call home." His comment just knocked me over. Serendipitously, I came across some excellent books on hospitality shortly thereafter. Once it hit me that Philip was describing hospitality, lots of implications and applications occurred to me. A few chapters into the project it dawned on me that hospitality is the antidote to commercialism. That was a very exciting discovery.

DW: *Commercialism seems to be on your mind. What's the problem with approaching adoption with a business mentality?*

JG: It *is* on my mind; I can't tell you how vigorously I grieve this trend. As dreadful as secrecy was, I think this commercial thing is worse. It's worse because it depersonalizes and dehumanizes a set of interpersonal interactions that cry out for respectful tenderness. The old secret-based system looked adoptive persons in the eye and told them they weren't entitled to basic information about themselves. That was awful, but now the commercial approach to adoption comes along and treats them like so many products to move about. How do you like that, children as products? Of course it's dressed up to look better than that, but when the clever packaging is stripped away, it's a business transaction. We know that it's a crime to sell a child—interesting, isn't it, that we assign so little responsibility to the purchaser? —but that doesn't stop us from chipping away at this taboo. We can buy or sell just about anything in our market-giddy world, but children? Are we okay with that? Are we okay with the idea that adoptive families are *consumers of children*? What a phrase that is, consumers of children. Put your nose in a dictionary and you'll find that to consume something is to destroy or devour it. There's some language for adoption, wouldn't you say?

Through the years I've done plenty of crabbing about the businessification of adoption, but it was futile because I couldn't articulate a constructive alternative. The language of openness that worked so well to counter secrecy doesn't work in the effort to rebut commercialism. If anything, as a school of thought that chafes against restriction, it may even play into commercialization! But here's what I've figured out. People are drawn to commercial adoption because it reduces the exercise to a matter of satisfying personal need. Put that way, it seems acceptable because there is nothing objectionable about trying to get one's needs met. It utterly fails as an approach to adoption, though, because adoption is never a unilateral matter. It's not a *personal* endeavor; it's inherently *interpersonal*. Every adoption affects a host of concerned people, and its healthier forms take that fact into account. The pursuit of self-interest is not an adequate approach to adoption because it is ulterior in its interaction with others; it uses them and subordinates their interests. All this means that hospitality is more than a pleasant way to go about the difficult work of adoption—*it is indispensable*. As the antithesis of unchecked selfishness, hospitality dignifies and humanizes the endeavor. After all, one doesn't acquire children; one adopts them, and the difference between these verbs is the warmth and love involved. So, now, as my grasp of hospitality principles deepens, I feel increasingly able to address the failings of commercial adoption. And I'm not just grumbling; I'm offering a richer, more child-centered model.

DW: *Are adoption contracts an outgrowth of commercialism?*

JG: The use of contracts emerged well before commercialization picked up any real steam. The impetus toward contractual adoption came out of Jeanne Etter's work in Oregon in the early 1980's. She championed a form of openness that featured mediated agreements between birth- and adoptive families. Her work had the long view in mind, and her forte was encouraging clarity of expectations between the families. As her approach promoted respectful interaction between them, it was not the least bit commercial.

DW: *While we're at it, how well do you think today's contracts jibe with hospitality?*

JG: Not very well, I'm afraid. As much as I like the effort that contractual adoption makes to bolster the standing of birthfamilies and to clarify the expectations participants have of each other, I find it inhospitably adult-centered. Contracts are about the rights of the adults involved. Maybe there are some truly child-centered contracts out there, but no one has brought any examples to my attention. Contracts put everything into concrete, measurable terms. That is the strength of that approach, but from the perspective of hospitality, it is also its weakness. Hospitality is a much more adaptable way to think about and work with adoptive relationships.

DW: *Is there anything to be learned from the business model?*

JG: Absolutely. You and I have talked about this through the years, and you've taught me that effective businesspeople are very, very deliberate in their efforts to understand the needs and interests of their clients and that they work hard to forge real connections with them. They make a science of this, and the result of their effort is, interestingly, quite hospitable. I'm afraid that a lot of us adoption professionals have been so concerned about getting our agenda across that we've been rather cavalier about really tuning into our clients. Certainly I've been guilty of that. We can also learn from the emphasis business puts on leadership. That's significant because I believe the role of the contemporary adoption service provider is best understood as leader. You really caught my attention many years back when you spoke of "leadership at every level." That phrase brought fresh focus to my work. I can lead for a while, but soon these families need to fly on their own. In the effort to get folks ready for the adventure of adoption, I try to rouse and release the leadership within them so they will take ownership of their relationships. This is especially important in working with adoptive parents because their term as hosts lasts so long. Someone needs to provide leadership and keep things moving. If no one else steps into the role of instigator, it falls to them; they are the default instigators. Anyway, when it comes to learning about leadership, the best information by far comes from the business world.

DW: *Moving on, does hospitality require a religious foundation?*

JG: Since I've made the case for hospitality by drawing on a number of religious sources, this is a more than fair question. Let me begin by noting there's really no other way to make the case for hospitality. You can't prove its value with research; there is no choice but to turn to wisdom literature. But back to the question, the short answer is no. Hospitality doesn't require religion. What it requires is a good heart, and it's my observation that good-heartedness is not necessarily linked to faith. In my experience, faith-based adoption programs range extravagantly in terms of the hospitality they offer. Some absolutely lead the way, but there are others that are among the quickest to judge participants and among the slowest to welcome their input. But enough said. I'll let people decide for themselves whether religion softens the heart and prompts loving interaction with others, particularly the stranger.

While we're on the subject, though, allow me to say a little more about the religious underpinnings of hospitality. I'm most familiar with the Christian tradition, but the question allows me to reflect on the rich Jewish concept of charity, *tzedaka*. I like the way a Catholic writer, Cynthia Churchill, puts it in an online commentary.

> The concept of charity is flawed when it refers to gifts given to others out of the magnanimity of our hearts. By contrast, the traditional Hebrew concept of giving is *tzedaka*, translated as justice or "doing the right thing." This means that what I give to another person is already, in all justice, his or her property. Up until now, the gift has been in my safekeeping. (n.d.)

If she has it right, then *tzedaka* is the perfect frame of mind and heart from which to begin the hospitious adoptive endeavor. It keeps me humble while it keeps my cohort's dignity intact. I like that it views the stranger as entitled. This is really important because we struggle with this dynamic in adoption. I'm not thinking so much about adoptive parents feeling morally authorized to take care of their children, though that is an extraordinarily important matter, as I am about birthparents feeling entitled to remain involved. Too often we act as if they are lucky to remain on the scene. We act as if they are beholden to the adoptive parents for this privilege when it seems to me it just might be the other way around. I've heard from too many adoptive parents who delighted in their connection to their child's birthfamily and listened to the frustrations of too many adoptive parents who lost access to the birthfamily to think otherwise. We fear that we will create confusion if we view birthfamilies as entitled, that we won't be clear about who is in charge. But that line of worry indicates we have a fearful understanding of the arrangement. The sort of entitlement we ought to be talking about is the child's entitlement. He or she is entitled to claim all of the significant people in his or her life. With that in mind, I see birthfamily entitlement as an extension of the youngster's entitlement. "Entitled" birthfamilies are those who conscientiously follow through because they take seriously the claims their children have on them.

DW: *Is hospitality another way to push men to the margins?*

JG: Oh my, I sure hope not! With women handling the social agenda in so many households, I can see why you ask. Still, it's a frightening question because I think the men of adoption are already on the margins, and I certainly don't want to take us further in that direction. I wonder if hidden away somewhere deep in this question is the premise that men are less socially capable than women? If so, I have to reject that thought. I can't abide the idea that men are apt to come up short in the hospitality department. In fact, in my experience, men often excel in meeting these challenges! For a variety of reasons, many seem less threatened about maintaining contact with the other family than a lot of the women involved. So, no, I don't think an emphasis on hospitality makes the experience more feminine. If anything, hospitality is a way for men to re-enter the experience. I'm deeply confident that, with just a bit of welcome, decent, friendly, gutsy men can be counted on to share the adventure. Among many other contributions, they often add some much-needed humor to the mix.

Perhaps the most important way to respond to this question is to raise a counter question: Do our current policies and procedures welcome males as full participants? My observation is that they do not. We are quick to decry their absence, but we seldom go an extra mile to garner their participation. I suspect the fault is at least as much ours as theirs. The point is, we need to be intentionally hospitable to men.

DW: *How do we do that? How can we be intentionally hospitable to the men involved in adoption?*

JG: Well, this is a large, important, and sometimes thorny subject, and I'm afraid I won't do it justice in this format. Nevertheless, I'll offer a few observations. The first thing we need to do is to recognize how important these guys are to their children. If this truth ever really sinks in, we won't be so quick to relegate them to the sidelines. Frequently we prejudge them. I can't tell you how many times I've erred in this department. It's easy to do. So often the expectant mother contemplating adoption is angry with her procreative partner, and it is common for her to describe him in some pretty nasty terms. Buying into her perception uncritically, I subsequently approach the fellow with a bit of trepidation only to discover time and again that he is an impressive person. Now, of course, there are times when she had it exactly right, but truly, many of these fellows are filled with concern and care, and so are their families. Many of them feel disrespected and are frustrated with the laws, with our practices, and with us. They are upset because they've been completely left out of the loop. They want to know what's going on, and they want a chance to voice their thoughts. Also, it's my experience that they want straight talk. By and large they don't have a lot of patience for euphemistic adoption jab-ber, and I think that's to their credit. In fact, I think they grow weary of all the talking we do in adoption. What a talky experience this can be! If we really want to involve the men of adoption, we need to get out of the office and out of the living room and go do things together. That works better for many of these guys.

While we're on this subject, allow me an offhand observation: I think we've seen some real progress through the years. I think guys are taking more interest in their children than they did when I was first involved with this work. This is no time to let up—there is a lot of ground still to gain—but I think we may be trending in a positive direction.

DW: *What's hospitality's impact on adoptive persons?*

JG: As mentioned earlier, if the hospitable approach takes hold, the kids are given a much greater role in fashioning their experience. I'm excited to anticipate the improved opportunities it creates for them, but I know it will create some additional burdens as well.

DW: *Burdens?*

JG: I think so. I think they will mostly be glad to have a voice, but we know that even as adults it isn't always easy to navigate our way through relationship networks. There are delicacies to weigh. Along these lines, for example, I've always been reluctant to put adoptive kids on the platform at adoption conferences. They're the ones everyone wants to hear from and they're a big hit whenever we give them the stage, but it's very tricky work for them. If they're up there whistling "Everything's wonderful in its own way," their account doesn't seem entirely credible. On the other hand, if they talk about their disappointments and frustrations, they feel like they're stepping on the toes of the people they love.

DW: *What's the impact on birthfamilies?*

JG: For starters, a caution comes to mind, a really important heads up. I think they need to be on the lookout for false hospitality. Pregnant women and couples pondering the possibility that their child might be best served by adoption will gain a cheerful reception anywhere they turn, but they need to realize that in some instances this positive response is ulterior and transitory. It's not easy to see through this sneaky friendliness, but they do well to proceed with caution and ask lots of discerning questions.

Something that stands out for me is how important it is that they select a hospitious adoptive family. If they are serious about honoring their child's claims on them and staying involved, they do well to choose adoptive parents for whom hospitality is second nature. An expectant mother comes to mind who wanted a family for her child that was hospitable, wealthy, and outspokenly religious. We had a very impressive family to offer—welcoming, well-off, and sincerely (though not aggressively) religious—but she passed on them in favor of a family she found elsewhere that was wealthy, outspokenly religious, and emotionally standoffish. She told us that she was miserable with worry about prospects for future contact, but that she clung to the hope that they might warm up as time went on. It was entirely her call to make, but I think she seriously undervalued the importance of hospitality and my hunch is that she is presently a stranger to her child.

Many of us have struggled to describe how birthfamilies fit into the story as it moves forward. In a previous book, *Lifegivers* [2000], I suggested it's not so much what they do as it is who they are. That remains true, but unfortunately that observation offers little interactive direction. I think hospitality can help birthfamilies get their bearings in this regard. In the best of circumstances, the connection between the participants grows into friendship or takes on a familial quality. When that's the case, folks know how to act because they know about friendship and they know about families. Roles are trickier when things remain more formal. In those instances, we do well to see each other as members of "the hospitality team," partners in the important work of helping the youngster feel at home in the world.

Another obvious implication is that we need to do a lot more to actively include important people we routinely—dare I say, systemically—overlook. We talked earlier about birthfathers, but I'm also talking about the youngster's siblings and grandparents and other members of the extended family. Somehow we need to find the time to help siblings and grandparents and uncles and aunts and influential friends find ways to meaningfully participate in these arrangements.

I think most birthfamilies long for higher levels of hospitality, but not all. My claim that the needs of children are best met by adoptions that feature hospitality directly challenges those birthfamilies who "just want to move on." I know that there can be times when the pain of continuing involvement seems too much to bear, and I am loathe to complicate an already grueling set of decisions. That said, I think we have sometimes let birthfamilies off the hospitality hook too easily. I am just as disappointed with birthfamilies who invoke privacy for the sake of personal convenience as I am with adoptive parents who take the easy path of disengagement.

One more quick thought occurs to me. As I reflect on the adoptive relationships I've had the chance to observe, they strike me as less reciprocal than we hoped they would be. The preponderance of interaction happens in adoptive parent territory. I think everyone would benefit if birthfamilies did more of the hosting.

DW: *What's the impact on adoptive families?*

JG: Hospitality certainly isn't the easiest way to go, but I'm sure it's the path of greatest satisfaction. When we first started bringing birth- and adoptive families together, we wondered if we were asking too much of our adoptive parents. What we soon learned is that they were our most enthusiastic participants. The fact is, most of them find the interaction enjoyable. That is an amazing thing to say given the theme of loss that runs though it all, but truly, people have fun in these arrangements. Maybe it sounds strange to hear me say that because I worry so about underplaying the difficulty of adoption, but let me say that again: Lots of people really enjoy these connections! Also, adoptive parents appreciate the endorsement so many of them receive from their child's birthfamily. It really feels good to them to know the birthfamily has their back.

A few lucky souls seem to fall into these hospitious relationships, but more often these connections are earned. The building of hospitable adoptive relationships requires risk-taking and emotional work. Surely it's easier not to notice, not to listen to all of those between-the-lines messages, not make room, but I think it feels pretty good to know that you've done all you can to help your child find his way. Conversely, I wonder how people live with the idea that in at least one important dimension of their child's life, they jettisoned their advocate role and shifted into a nervous neutral.

DW: *What's the impact on service providers?*

JG: Hospitality requires the courage to buck convention. Most professional models encourage us to keep a safe distance from those we would serve, but hospitality doesn't allow us that kind of cover. To the contrary, it asks us to find ways to be more fully available. Availability means allowing ourselves to be known, being physically on hand at key moments, and encountering the full range of emotions stirred by the process. That's a tall order because every proposed adoption will produce a family that gains and a family that loses. Each time we set out on one of these ventures, I know that someone is going to be delighted and someone else will be coping with indescribable pain. It's a lot more comfortable to lay low in the office than to be on the scene in the midst of all those emotions. It requires other sorts of courage, too. We need the courage to be unproductively involved. That is to say, there will be times when we are simply with people and have little educational or therapeutic purpose other than being there. When I'm in that mode I sometimes think, "Whoa, I hope no one is watching." Importantly, we need the courage to stay in touch with hope-filled families even when there is no news to share and their discouragement and impatience is palpable. We need the courage to get out of the way when we're at risk to crowd people or when we're at risk to intrude on emotionally intimate moments between participants. All this making room is pretty tough for those of us who feel pressure to keep things under control and to be doing things. We also need the courage to honor our best intuitions and hospitiously speak our truth to the powerbrokers around us. I really like how Parker Palmer puts this in the afterward to the anniversary edition of *The Courage to Teach*. He writes,

> In the midst of the powerful force field of institutional life, where so much might compromise my core values, I have found firm ground on which to stand—the ground of my

own identity and integrity, of my own soul—ground from
which I can call myself, my colleagues and my workplace
back to our true mission. (2007, p. 213)

Nothing easy about that, is there? I am very confident that the
professionals reading this book will resonate with his words, but the
lousy truth is most of us are lodged in systems that are more interested in productivity than hospitality. Many are in a really tough
spot, and I'm a little concerned that this book will fuel some of those
fires. This clash between personal integrity and the demands of the
system is very difficult to manage. Sometimes we succeed in calling
the system to a higher level of service and sometimes the system
drives good people out of the field. It's a scary thing to put your
job on the line.

Even though I think most of us doing this work are naturally hospitious, there's reason to believe that we've not done very well in
creating hospitable systems. What I'm getting at is the rise of the
Safe Haven laws around the country. These laws are of concern on
several levels, but one conclusion I draw is that they are a sorry commentary on the lack of hospitality we've offered in our service networks. If we were known for our warm welcome and nonjudgmental
acceptance, people in desperate situations would feel freer to turn to
us and there would be less need for laws of this sort.

DW: *What does hospitality not address?*

JG: Hospitality moves things in the right direction, but it does not
ensure successful adoption. There are many complicated adoptive
situations where the participants are going to need specialized assistance in order to find their way through. For all its grace and beauty,
hospitality does not cure mental illness or substance abuse. Also,
what are we to do with capable but intensely private, insular people
who wish to be involved in adoption but who are disinclined
toward hospitality? If we believe that hospitality is essential to
child-centered adoption, where do they fit in?

DW: *What's the downside of hospitality?*

JG: It has to be the work it requires. Don't we all wish things could be simple and relatively effortless? We typically try to avoid the difficult path, especially when we're really overloaded and tired. There are plenty of times when it's hard to find the energy to be fully available. And making things all the tougher, there is no guarantee that our efforts will bear any fruit.

DW: *What are some of the common misunderstandings of hospitality?*

JG: There are many. Perhaps the most common is that it's about table etiquette and lightweight pleasantries. Another is that it's spineless, that it's some kind of doormat routine. People who practice the art of hospitality are amused by that one because they know how much backbone is involved. A common error is to think of hospitality as an event or two rather than a way of life. Some dismiss it as inconsequential. In reality, hospitality is a deeper and richer and more universally respected tradition than most of us realize.

DW: *What don't we usually get about hospitality?*

JG: Most of us think that the hard part is setting and enforcing boundaries, but I think the most difficult part is to get over the tendency to judge. I know for me, at least, this is tough. I fear I'm better at keeping others at an arm's length than I am at wrapping my arms around them and drawing them in. I also think it's really, really difficult to give people the room they need and not crowd them. I fancy myself so full of good ideas and problem solving and advice that I'm often intrusive without even realizing it. It's really difficult to become engaged and to care, yet to tread lightly.

DW: *Is there such a thing as partial hospitality?*

JG: It seems odd to me to speak of half-hearted hospitality. Ultimately, it's a plunge we take, but I suppose many of us stick one toe in the water at a time and we grow into hospitality incrementally. Falling into this category of partial hospitality are those situations where some party or another, who might have a lot of interest in the situation if they knew about it, is intentionally left out of the adoption. Sometimes this happens for reasons of safety, other times because of anger or shame. However it happens, when exclusion is built into the plan, everyone has to work within these limits. It's often awkward, it often feels inhospitable—dishonest, even—and it often frustrates the kids as they grow older. I know there are times when it is very, very tempting to leave some abrasive people out of the planning because they are sure to make an already difficult situation even more difficult, but, in my experience, it's best to resist this temptation. These front-end shortcuts have a way of turning into even bigger headaches later on.

DW: *Can one go about hospitality unilaterally?*

JG: Ah, this question brings up the all too common sadness of unrequited hospitality. The answer, of course, is yes. In fact, since authentic hospitality is offered with no strings attached, I suppose we should always think of it as unilateral. Hospitality is an offering, not a gambit in search of exchange, but I must admit that this selfless ideal is probably seldom accomplished. Most of the time we're not just extending a helpful hand, we're making a bid for connection. When connection is not established or sustained, we take it personally. We need to be careful in our thinking about this because there is something off-base about imposing expectations in the name of hospitality. It doesn't make sense to talk about pushy hospitality. We can make ourselves available and invite others to join us in an exciting journey, but their course of action is always up to them. All we can do is hold up our end. Hospitality is certainly more dynamic when it is reciprocal, but I believe we can meaningfully acknowledge others without their cooperation. Even so, I grieve that there are many wonderful participants who are frustrated because their hospitable overtures were rebuffed.

DW: *So, what do they do with this frustration? How does a parent hospitably comment on the inhospitable actions of the other parents?*

JG: The word that comes to mind is *grace*. How else do we handle frustration? Whether the relationship is operational or not, I believe the others involved are essential partners in raising the youngster. If your partner is uncooperative and unavailable and your child suffers, it's maddening. Somehow, for the child's sake, this frustration has to be forgiven. I'm not unsympathetic to their exasperation, but we all know that bridge-building attitudes and behaviors produce better results than tantrums.

DW: *What should parents do when the kids act inhospitably?*

JG: No matter how much we believe in it, hospitality ought not be heavy-handed. We can't make our kids act hospitably. Most of the time the wisest course is to try to understand what is blocking the genial path. Hospitality, after all, has many enemies. To mention a few: fear, stubbornness, judgment, and anger all get in the way. Parents can help kids work on these impediments. To an extent, hospitality can be taught, but ultimately it's a matter of the heart.

DW: *Might some kids get carried away with the hospitable opportunities provided by their well-meaning parents?*

JG: This is a very important question. First, let me say again that the idea here is not that the kids rule the roost. The adults need to establish clear and reasonable boundaries commensurate with each child's capacity to handle fluid circumstances. Next, although I probably wouldn't use the expression "carried away," it's clear that some kids are far more interested in exercising connections to their first family than others. Some kids enjoy really great chemistry with their birthfamily. They just light up when they are around them, and it's something to behold. Given the opportunity to safely express their interests and wishes, I expect those kids will emote a lot of positive impressions and promote *lots* of interaction. I don't know how that observation hits people. Some may think it's great and others may think it sounds frightening. Well, like it or not, some adoptive kids viscerally connect to their birthfamily, so we need to deal with that reality. And it's not the easiest family dynamic to come to terms with! It's exciting, but it is also very challenging. In some ways I think it leaves everybody a little sad. It leads adoptive parents to wonder if they have somehow intruded on nature's intentions, and it can gen-erate feelings of insecurity in even the most loving of them. It adds weight to the normal but heavy question birthfamilies have to come to terms with: namely, did they make the right call when they entrusted their child to the care of another family? And worst of all, it can stir notions in a child's mind that a mistake has been made and that he just needs to put in some time before he can straighten things out and get back to "his people."

The idea of kids biding their time as they grow up breaks my heart. A predictable temptation arises. If the connection to biologic kin stirs sadness or insecurity, might it be best to throttle back on the interactive pace? That's an understandable impulse, but experience suggests that inclusive responses bring better results. Nothing good comes from frustrating these youngsters. If we communicate that they are wrong to be so interested in their first family, we drive them crazy. If we forbid contact, it's as if we issued them a dare; they end up more resolved than ever to seek out their birthfamily. Backpedaling serves no one well; adoption does not shine when it becomes an either/or proposition that cuts children off from loved ones. And I'm concerned that adoptive parents will lose out over the long haul if they shut things down. It's better to retain access to the emotions involved than to drive them underground, and it's bet-ter to huddle with the birthfamily to fashion a coherent response than to react unilaterally. Having said all that, let's not kid ourselves. The hospitious response asks a great deal of parents, especially in these circumstances, and I give those who affirm and bless their child's vigorous interest in his birthfamily a world of credit. That's a brave expression of sacrificial parental love.

DW: *What happens when hospitality really works?*

JG: Hospitality opens doors, and it gets things going. It has a way of helping things cohere. Once it has worked its initial magic, though, it slips into the background. That is to say, in high compatibility and high courage situations, hospitality is gradually replaced with the relatedness of friendship or with a sense of having become extended family. When relationships take hold at this more committed level, the dynamic of guest and host gives way to a higher level of intimacy and, interestingly, healthy presumption. These are exciting families to be around.

DW: *My guess is that most people do pretty well in those first few meetings because everyone is so motivated to makes things work. What Julie and I discovered as we moved forward with our adoptions is that there needs to be a second, more profound version of acceptance. This deeper hospitality finds ways to welcome that which is difficult and unpredictable. It's a leap of faith that says, "I'm not entirely sure what makes you tick, and, to be frank, some of what you seem to be about worries me. Nevertheless, you are without doubt important to my child, and that makes you important to me. So bring it on! Enter my life, and be who you are." Can you comment on this deeper hospitality?*

JG: Well said! I doubt I can add much to what you've shared. You're definitely on to something with this idea of "deeper hospitality," and you've gone right to the heart of the matter when you speak of welcoming "that which is difficult." You've put your finger on the pivot point where some pretty fine people bail out. They're okay with everything until that juncture is reached, but then they shut down. I think if they could join the conversation they would tell us that this is a bridge too far. They would say that it's nuts to welcome difficulty, that they have enough difficulty in their lives without welcoming more, and I have to admit that their complaint makes a lot of sense. No easy answers to this one; just tons of soul searching. I very much like the way you put it just now. Moving ahead really is a leap of faith. It's the faith that between us there is enough goodwill and savvy to find a workable way to stay connected. For the sake of our kids, we'll do things we would never do otherwise.

DW: *It's a learning experience each time out—for the professionals—but especially for the principals. The idea of hospitality is foundational, but the circumstances are unique and specific.*

JG: So true. There's so much trial and error involved. No one really masters hospitality. We can get a handle on some of the larger dynamics, but it comes to life in the details. And as you've noted, the details are never the same. That means we are all students. When we come together and share our experiences, we become a learning community. I find that exciting. Given all the discovery that is going on, I don't see how we could ever grow smug.

DW: *Do you have any suggestions to help families manage their differences?*

JG: A range of suggestions is offered in the chapter on differences, Chapter 8, and I'm hoping just about everyone will find there an idea or two or 10 that they can put to work. Your question brings to mind an observation I've heard our wise friend, Sharon Roszia, make on different occasions. She reminds folks that it is a mistake to treat adoptive relationships as if they are somehow different from others. She points out that there's a good chance that the challenge of the moment has been encountered in prior relationships, and goes on to ask, "How did you work with Uncle Charley when he pulled that same sort of stunt?" I think that's a very sensible and practical way for us to find our way.

DW: *Staying with the subject of differences, does hospitality have implications for international adoption?*

JG: I'm glad for this question because I think some people intentionally head down the international trail as a way to dodge the birthfamily and hospitality challenges built into domestic adoption. They think international adoption is birthparentless. If that's what they have in mind, I am pretty sure they are in for some big surprises. I say this because an "out of sight, out of mind" approach to birthfamilies seriously underestimates the importance that thoughtful adoptive persons attach to their origins. Parents with no access to their child's birthrelatives have their work cut out for them. I believe there is a very strong chance that these parents will discover that the skills of hospitality—noticing, listening, and making room—are more important than ever when adopting internationally. Hospitality in the abstract may very well be more difficult to work through than is face-to-face hospitality. Adoptive parents will need the eyes of hospitality to notice birthparents when they are only present in spirit. They will need hospitious ears to hear their child's veiled questions and yearnings on these matters. They will need accepting and imaginative hearts as they fill in for and cover for their unknown and unavailable partners.

To my way of thinking, this under-valuation of rootedness is a throwback to the days when domestic adoptions were all secret. In that version of adoption, birthfamilies were considered inconsequential and were relegated to the shadows. Even so, some adoptive parents found ways to at least emotionally include them. Colleen Ramsey, an adoptive mother from Nebraska, comes to mind. She tells of stealing into her son's bedroom to give him a birthday kiss after a long day of celebration. With the festivities of the day behind him, he slept contentedly. Tucking him into the covers, she kissed him once and then kissed him again, the second on behalf of his birthmother, whom she knew surely ached for him that very moment. I believe this remembrance was a sacred act of hospitality.

Returning to the challenges of international adoption, it goes without saying that cross-cultural circumstances require lots of hospitality. With the travel involved, everyone's out of his or her element, so it's important to notice and listen intently. Homework pays off, too, so we can keep our blunders to a minimum and demonstrate our interest in and respect for this culture we hope to join. Since adoption takes adopters into some of a nation's most forgotten corners, places where circumstances can be pretty grim, respect is enormously important. Language barriers complicate interaction, but happily, there is something about the hospitable spirit that transcends language.

Much more could and should be said, but let me just offer the caution that parents adopting internationally need to be very careful in the way they handle their child's story. It's tempting to focus on the deprivations the youngster endured because they justify his adoption. My concern is that this may fuel a child's sense of shame about his origins. Better, I think, that we guard our commentary and simply offer the observation that we knew from the moment we first met that this was a spectacular child and that we were astonishingly fortunate to add him to our family.

DW: *What do you recommend to someone who wants to learn more about hospitality?*

JG: Just go for it! The best way to get better at hospitality is to dive in and do it. With experience, our fears usually shrink. If a little more fortifying is necessary, though, before taking the plunge, a couple of things occur to me. One is to do some reading. Happily, there is a growing body of literature about hospitality. The two books that impressed and inspired me the most were Christine Pohl's *Making Room* and Daniel Homan and Lonni Collins Pratt's *Radical Hospitality*. Better yet, spend a little time with the natural masters of hospitality in your life and watch them closely. I mean really study them, because their art is so subtle. How do they do it? How do they communicate their interest and acceptance?

DW: *Did writing this book affect you in any way?*

JG: No doubt. I am much more mindful of hospitality than I used to be; I see the need for it almost everywhere I look. Mother Teresa observed that the greatest disease humans face is that of being unwanted. But I hasten to add that for all my research on the subject, I'm still not very good at it. I believe I'm quite a bit better at describing it and making the case for it than I am at getting it done. I just hope my liabilities bring no discredit to the concept. My favorite spiritual writer, Henri Nouwen, wrestled with this problem in his time. In *Bread for the Journey* he wrote,

> Can we only speak when we are fully living what we are saying? If all our words had to cover all our actions, we would be doomed to permanent silence! Sometimes we are called to proclaim God's love even when we are not yet fully able to live it. Does that mean we are hypocrites? Only when our own words no longer call us to conversion. Nobody completely lives up to his or her own ideals and visions. But by proclaiming our ideals and visions with great conviction and humility, we may gradually grow into the truth we speak. (1997)

So that's my hope in all this—that I will gradually grow into the truth of hospitality.

DW: *Any last words?*

JG: I don't know about you, but sometimes I end up a little frustrated when I finish a book that made a lot of sense to me. "Great ideas," I think, "but what good are they? I'm not wired for that sort of grand gesture; the sorry truth is that these notions are well beyond my reach." Well, the beauty of hospitality is that it is entirely doable. Each small act of noticing, listening, and making room makes a difference. So that's the last word: We can do this.

REFERENCES

Arendt, Hannah. (1956). *The Human Condition*. Chicago: University of Chicago Press.

Benne, Robert. (1998, October). "Abortion—Moral and Legal Reflections." *The Cresset, 62*(1). Reformation.

Burgess, Linda Cannon. (1976). *The Art of Adoption*. Washington, DC: Acropolis Books.

Churchill, Cynthia. (n.d.). "Tzedaka," *The Catholic Worker Movement*. Reprinted from *Workers and Friends* (1996, Winter). Champaign, IL: St. Jude Catholic Worker Community. Available online at http://catholicworker.org/roundtable/essaytext.cfm?Number=8.

de Béthune, Pierre-François. (2002). *By Faith and Hospitality: The Monastic Tradition as a Model for Interreligious Encounter*. Eastbourne, England: Gracewing.

Derrida, Jacques. (2001). *Cosmopolitanism and Forgiveness*. New York: Routledge.

Doyle, Brian. (2003). *Leaping: Revelations and Epiphanies*. Chicago: Loyola Press.

Faulkner, William. (1973). *Flags in the Dust*. New York: Random House.

Gritter, James. (Ed.). (1989). *Adoption Without Fear*. San Antonio: Corona.

Gritter, James. (2000). *Lifegivers: Framing the Birthparent Experience in Open Adoption*. Washington, DC: CWLA Press.

Guenther, Margaret. (1992). *Holy Listening: The Art of Spiritual Direction*. Cambridge: Cowley.

Guiness, Os. (1998). *The Call: Finding and Fulfilling the Central Purpose of Your Life*. Nashville: Word.

Gunderson, Gary. (1997). *Deeply Woven Roots: Improving the Quality of Life in Your Community*. Minneapolis: Fortress Press.

Homan, Daniel and Pratt, Lonni Collins. (2002). *Radical Hospitality: Benedict's Way of Love*. Brewster, MA: Paraclete Press.

James, Henry. (Ed.). (1926). *The Letters of Williams James Vol. 2*. Boston: Atlantic Monthly Press.

Kinnamon, Michael. (1999, July 16). *Welcoming the Stranger*. Presentation at the Many Faces of the Spirit conference, Lexington, KY. Available online at www.uga.edu/bahai/News/071699.html.

Kirk, H. David. (1964). *Shared Fate: A Theory of Adoption and Mental Health*. New York: The Free Press.

Love: The Words and Inspiration of Mother Teresa. (2007). Boulder, CO: Blue Mountain Press.

Lynch, Thomas. (2005). *Booking Passage: We Irish & Americans*. New York: W. W. Norton.

Manning, Brendan. (2002). *The Wisdom of Tenderness*. New York: HarperSanFrancisco.

Melina, Lois, and Roszia, Sharon. (1993). *The Open Adoption Experience*. New York: HarperCollins.

Merton, Thomas. (2000). *Essential Writings*. Maryknoll, NY: Orbis.

Merton, Thomas, and Bochen, Christine. (Ed.). (1997). *The Journals of Thomas Merton, Vol. 6*. New York: HarperSanFrancisco.

"New Adoption Study Shows Direct Contact Between Adoptive Families and Birthmothers Results in Greater Birthmother Satisfaction." (2002, Oct. 7). Austin, TX: The University of Texas at Austin. Available online at www.utexas.edu/news/2002/10/7/nr_adoption.

Nouwen, Henri. (1975). *Reaching Out: The Three Movements of the Spiritual Life*. Garden City, NY: Doubleday.

Nouwen, Henri. (1994). *With Burning Hearts*. Maryknoll, NY: Orbis Books.

Nouwen, Henri. (1997). *Bread for the Journey*. New York: HarperSanFrancisco.

Oden, Amy. (2001). *And You Welcomed Me: A Sourcebook on Hospitality in Early Christianity*, Nashville: Abingdon Press.

Palmer, Parker. (1997). *In the Company of Strangers*. New York: Crossroad.

Palmer, Parker. (2007, 10th Anniversary ed.). *The Courage to Teach*. San Francisco: Jossey-Bass.

Pavao, Joyce Maguire. (2004, August 9). Interview by Spaulding for Children. Laguna Beach, CA.

Peterson, Eugene. (1991). *Where Your Treasure Is*. Grand Rapids, MI: Eerdmans.

Pohl, Christine. (1999). *Making Room: Recovering Hospitality as a Christian Tradition*. Grand Rapids, MI: Eerdmans.

Reynolds, Thomas E. (2008). *Vulnerable Communion: A Theology of Disability and Hospitality*. Grand Rapids, MI: Eerdmans.

Richard, Lucien. (2000). *Living the Hospitality of God*. Mahwah, NJ: Paulist Press.

Roszia, Sharon. (2004, August 9). Interview by Spaulding for Children. Laguna Beach, CA.

Schneider, Carl. (1997). *Shame, Exposure, and Privacy*. New York: W.W. Norton & Company.

Sennett, Richard. (2003). *Respect in a World of Inequality*. New York: Norton.

Severson, Randolph. (1991). *Charms and Rituals for Healing*. Dallas: House of Tomorrow.

Severson, Randolph. (1994). *Philosophy and Experience*. Dallas: House of Tomorrow.

Severson, Randolph. (1998). *Spiritual Existential Counseling*. Dallas: Bosobel.

Smedes, Lewis. (1982). *How Can It Be Alright When Everything Is All Wrong?* New York: Harper & Row.

Smith, Susan. (1993, Winter). "Co-Creating the Household of God: Two Models of Hospitality." *Benedictines*. Kansas City, KS: Mount St. Scholastica.

Taylor, Barbara Brown. (2000). *The Luminous Web*. Boston: Cowley.

Tutu, Desmond. (2004). *God Has a Dream: A Vision of Hope for Our Time*. New York: Doubleday.

Volf, Miroslav. (1996). *Exclusion and Embrace: A Theological Exploration of Identity, Otherness, and Reconciliation.* Nashville: Abingdon.

Volf, Miroslav, and Bass, Dorothy. (2002). *Practicing Theology: Beliefs and Practices in Christian Life*. Grand Rapids, MI: Eerdmans.

Webster's New International Dictionary. (2nd ed.). (1944). Springfield, MA: G. & C. Merriam.

Webster's New International Dictionary. (3rd ed.). (1965). Springfield, MA: G. & C. Merriam.

Wolf, Daniel. (2007). *Prepared and Resolved: The Strategic Agenda for Growth, Performance, and Change*. Grand Rapids, MI: dsb Publishing.

Wolff, Jana. (1st ed.). (1997). *Secret Thoughts of an Adoptive Mother.* Kansas City, MO: Andrews and McMeel.

York, Sarah. (2002). *The Holy Intimacy of Strangers*. San Francisco: JoseyBass.

ACKNOWLEDGMENTS

Over the years people have wondered how a little agency in northern Michigan, Catholic Human Services, came to be a place where openness could flourish. Perhaps the thing that set us apart was our hospitality, or more precisely, our willingness to receive hospitality from the people we hoped to serve. The outfit has always been more interested in connecting with others than in keeping them at a professional arm's length. That culture of connection positioned us to listen to and learn from adoption's foremost experts, the families who were exploring and testing adoption's capacities on a daily basis. I am forever indebted to our program's early champions— the Vander Haagens, Sprys, Romanchiks, Lundys, Beckwiths, Spinnikens, Thomases, Dombroskis, and Vander Kolks, to mention just a few—who bought into our approach well before we were able to articulate an adequate rationale for our innovations. They didn't need any persuading; hospitality was in their bones, and they were ready to live it out. Our task as social workers was to push the institutional boundaries back a little so these good-hearted folks had room to hospitate. Given the chance to do adoption in a way that made sense to them, they brought great creativity and warmth to the adventure. With simple grace and courage, they demonstrated the considerable potential of hospitious adoption.

I can only write about hospitality because I've received so much of it. It's come my way in many forms. A lot of it has been fun. Birthgrandfather Mike Romanchik's invitation to join him for a Pistons game when I was stuck a long way from home comes to mind. Some of it was tasty. I'll not soon forget the devastating chocolate pecan pie at the Goloviches', the wonderful Indian cuisine at the Mishras', or Marc Cesario's astounding hamburgers. Often it was moving. Countless families have welcomed me to share in milestone events—graduations, weddings, baptisms, anniversaries, and funerals—as well as small-yet-revealing moments of everyday family life. Apart from these generous acts of inclusion, I would know little about the transforming power of hospitality. As their feats of hospitality far exceed my powers of description, this book only hints at their greatness.

I am thankful that CWLA made room for this volume in their slate of publications. Their stellar reputation lends weight to a perspective that some might otherwise think too novel to take seriously. And even though editor Meghan Williams set aside my description of home as the "belongiest" place one would ever know, I greatly appreciate her skillful handling of the manuscript. She was good to it and to me throughout the project.

I am grateful to the staff at Catholic Human Services. With administrators David Martin and Becky Wagner leading the way, the hospitality of this capable crew is hardly surprising. Colleague Doree Kent followed the book's progress with interest and offered helpful clarifications along the way. My longtime adoption sidekick, Abbie Nelson, is a natural master of hospitality. Disarming and often comical, she has a keen eye for the person who is not fitting in so well. If you took the hospitality out of Abbie, there would be nothing left.

Some of the hospitality I've encountered in my journey strikes me as especially surprising and extravagant. How did it ever happen that I am able to count adoption's royalty—Annette Baran, Reuben Pannor, Joyce Maguire Pavao, and Sharon Roszia—as friends? They, and so many other experts too numerous to identify, extended great hospitality and kindness through the years and taught me a great deal as we toiled with common purpose. Infant mental health specialist Michael Trout generously gave the "Gentle Transition" chapter a close and meticulous reading. Many thanks to Dan Wolf who affirmed and expanded this project from start to finish. His enthusiastic early commentary led me to believe that hospitality was a theme worth developing. And, of course, I appreciate his willingness to play the intrepid Mr. Question to my queasy Mr. Answer in the final chapter. Randy Severson remains the most interesting voice in adoption. His friendship is a gift that I treasure, and I am amazed and humbled by his most gracious Foreword.

Of course, the best of the hospitality is always close to home. For putting up with all the inconvenience and commotion that goes with the writing of a book, I thank my good wife, Liz.

ABOUT THE AUTHOR

James L. Gritter MSW was the child welfare supervisor at Catholic Human Services in Traverse City, Michigan, for more than 30 years. Named a Social Work Pioneer by the National Association of Social Workers and an Angel in Adoption by Congress, he is a recipient of the Baran-Pannor Award for Excellence in Open Adoption. His previous books include *Adoption Without Fear*, which he edited, as well as *The Spirit of Open Adoption* (CWLA Press, 1997) and *Lifegivers: Framing the Birthparent Experience in Open Adoption* (CWLA Press, 2000). He and his wife live in Williamsburg, Michigan.